A Guide for Family, Friends, and Allies
of the Deaf and Hard of Hearing

Becoming

AN EMPOWERED HEARING ALLY

Katherine S. Rybak

HEARING OUT LOUD
BOOKS

Cover Design: Kaitlin Walsh of Lyon Road Art

For permission requests and ordering information, email the author at:
katherine@hearingoutloud.net

ISBN: 979-8-9941134-2-4

For more information about the author, to book her for your next event,
media interview, or bulk orders, please contact her at:
katherine@hearingoutloud.net

a letter to the reader

To the Ally Who's Ready to Listen,

You picked up this book because someone in your life has hearing loss, and you want to support them. That choice already makes you an ally. An "ally" simply means someone who chooses to show up with curiosity and compassion—regardless of the role you play in their life. Being an ally isn't about having all the answers; it's about being willing to learn and adjust.

Communication is a shared responsibility. When you prepare yourself to engage with intention and respond with understanding, you make genuine connection possible.

Your effort matters more than perfection. Every step you take helps ease isolation and lets the person you care about know they are not alone.

Thank you for showing up,

Katherine

For my own allies—

To Carol, my wife and closest ally, whose love, patience, and strength
have carried me through every challenge.

To my children—Alex, Danielle, Kenzie, and son-in-law Kevin—
thank you for growing alongside me, adapting, learning, and
reminding me that connection is always worth the effort.

To my dad, David Rybak,
my very first ally, who showed me what steadfast support looks like.

To my sister, Christine Rybak, and to Nina Buchanan—
thank you for listening, encouraging, and standing beside me
with understanding hearts.

And to my granddaughters, Roan Mary and Breen—
thank you for your curiosity, kindness,
and the way you already ask the right questions.

contents

1 | preparation

Overview

This book is designed to be read and applied at your own pace. Each chapter combines instructional content, ally applications, reflection prompts, and optional tie-ins that connect to your communication partner's guided journal (*Becoming Hearing Empowered*), if they are using that book.

Do move through the chapters in order, because each chapter builds understanding for the next. You might spend a week on each of the eight chapters, finishing the book in about two months. Or take it more slowly, pausing when a chapter feels especially personal or when you want to practice the applications more deeply. Some readers set aside a weekend or retreat-style block of time to dive in more intensively.

This book also works well in a community. Consider joining or starting a book club with other allies, family members, or friends of people with hearing loss.

Throughout this book, you'll see references to additional resources.

Check out **hearingoutloud.net/resources** for helpful links to videos, organizations, hearing device manufacturers, assistive technology, and a free book group facilitator's guide.

This Is Not Therapy

This book is a powerful tool for reflection and growth, but it is not a replacement for professional support. Hearing loss stirs up strong emotions, not just for the person living with it, but for you too. If you find yourself struggling with intense sadness, fear, anxiety, or other emotional challenges, please seek help from a qualified therapist, such as a licensed social worker, psychologist, or psychiatrist.

The intent of this book is to provide knowledge, guidance, and exercises that strengthen your role as an ally. It's about building skills, reframing experiences, and walking alongside your friend with compassion. If you ever feel overwhelmed, remember that finding professional support is valuable and empowering in and of itself.

Optional: An Empowering Book for Your Loved One

Alongside this book, my previously mentioned book *Becoming Hearing Empowered: A Guided Journal for the Deaf and Hard of Hearing* is written directly for people living with hearing loss. It invites them to reflect on their experiences, learn about hearing science, practice self-advocacy, and process the emotions that come with communication challenges.

Your friend with hearing loss might choose to work in that journal while you reflect through this ally book, creating parallel opportunities for shared understanding and conversation. The chapters and sections coincide between the two books, and there are opportunities for you to offer support every step of the way. If they aren't ready for *Becoming Hearing Empowered*, that's okay; this book stands on its own. The knowledge, strategies, and insights you gain here will still strengthen your role as an ally and improve your relationship.

If your communication partner chooses to work through *Becoming Hearing Empowered* while you are working in *Becoming an Empowered Hearing Ally,* understanding what that experience looks like will help you support them well.

Becoming Hearing Empowered is

- **Transformative** – It challenges internalized stigma, encourages reframing negative experiences, and applies growth mindset and cognitive behavioral therapy (CBT) strategies.
- **Educational** – It explains hearing science, testing, and technology, helping them better understand their own hearing loss and options for support.
- **Emotionally intense** – It asks the person with hearing loss to revisit painful experiences of exclusion, frustration, or shame. This process may bring up sadness, grief, anger, or vulnerability.
- **Creative and reflective** – It uses writing, drawing, and color as tools for self-expression, which makes the work both therapeutic and draining.
- **Positive** – Some sections highlight identity, pride, resilience, and joy.

Important Landmarks in This Book

- ALLY PERSPECTIVE: Why This Matters: At the beginning of every section, these short intro paragraphs explain why the upcoming information matters for you.

- ALLY IN ACTION: Practical, concrete strategies and behaviors you can begin to use now.

- ALLY INSIGHTS: Guided reflection questions for you to consider what you have read and how it impacts your relationship.

- ALLY CONNECTION: BECOMING HEARING EMPOWERED: Direct tie-ins to the *Becoming Hearing Empowered* book that connects you with your loved one's reflections if they are working through the guided journal.

A Note on Your Own Capacity

Before we go further, I want to acknowledge something: allyship is emotional labor. Reading about hearing loss, examining your own patterns, and learning new strategies takes energy. You may feel tired. You may feel defensive. You may need to put this book down and come back later.

That's not failure. It's pacing. Your loved one doesn't need a perfect ally. They need a present one. If a chapter feels heavy, bookmark it. Return when you're ready. This book will wait for you.

Introduction

"You don't listen to me."

My wife's voice was calm, but I heard the hurt underneath. She had told me something important the night before—a change in plans for the next day, a time we needed to leave—and when the moment came, I had no memory of it. I'd been standing right there. I'd nodded. I'd said "okay." And yet the information was gone, as if she'd never spoken at all.

I wanted to explain, but I didn't have the words. I knew that if someone gets my attention first, I can more easily understand what's being said. But that evening, after a full day of straining to follow conversations, my brain was already spent. She'd told me while I was in the kitchen, probably while I was doing something else, probably without first making sure I was ready to listen. And I hadn't known how to ask for that. I didn't have the language to explain: *I need you to get my attention. Wait until I confirm I'm with you. Then tell me the important thing.*

So we argued in circles. She felt invisible. I felt falsely accused. She thought I wasn't trying. I thought she didn't understand how hard I *was* trying. The real culprit was my hearing loss. By evening, my brain was running on empty. All my mental energy had gone into just decoding broken sounds into words, leaving nothing left for actually remembering them. But we didn't know that's what was happening.

It took years for us to build the routine we have now. Years of circular arguments before I could finally articulate what I needed: *Get my attention. Wait for me to look at you. Then share the important information.* It sounds so simple. But I didn't have the words for it, and she didn't know to ask.

That argument has happened more than once in our house. Maybe it's happened in yours, too.

This book exists so you don't have to wait years to find the words.

Why I Wrote This Book

I've lived with progressive hearing loss since childhood. I've worked as a Teacher of the Deaf and Hard of Hearing. I've facilitated groups where adults share struggles most hearing people never witness: the stigma, the fatigue, the isolation.

One message comes through again and again: *"My family and friends don't really understand what this feels like."*

I'm honored to walk alongside you in these pages as we explore what it means to become an empowered hearing ally.

For me, the challenge was never only about missing sounds. It was the feeling of being different. Of not being understood. I still remember getting my first hearing aid in elementary school, the standard "silly putty beige" that was supposed to be "invisible" in my ear. I tried to make light of it by calling it anything but a hearing aid. I knew that hearing aids weren't considered "cool." Even as a child, I felt the pressure that hearing loss was something to hide. I didn't have words for it, but now I know what I was feeling: stigma. Shame about something that should never have been hidden.

Over the years, what made the difference wasn't just technology or strategies, it was the people around me. The times I felt most connected were when family, friends, or colleagues were willing to listen, adjust, and truly try to understand. The times I felt most alone were when they didn't. I know how much an ally's support, or lack of it, shapes the experience of hearing loss.

The truth is, hearing loss is profoundly isolating. Adults who develop hearing loss frequently have no other person who understands the experience. On average, people delay nine years from diagnosis to obtaining their first hearing aid, largely because of stigma. Nine years of struggling in conversations, bluffing through misunderstandings, and quietly withdrawing from social life. A few "never mind" moments are enough to make someone stop trying altogether.

I wrote *Becoming Hearing Empowered* because I know firsthand how hard it is to live with hearing loss. For years, I struggled with the stigma, the exhaustion of bluffing through conversations, and the quiet grief of feeling left out. Each change in my hearing forced me to figure out how to keep going, usually just muddling through it alone. I wanted to create the book I wish I'd had earlier. A place to process the emotions, learn practical strategies, and discover that hearing loss is not something to hide, but a part of who we are. Since its release, people have told me that it put words to feelings they could never explain, helped them feel less alone, and gave them the courage to face their hearing loss with new strength.

But hearing loss does not affect only the person who lives with it. It also affects the people around them: their family, their friends, and their coworkers. My own allies don't do this perfectly; we still get frustrated, miscommunicate, or hurt each other's feelings. But we've learned that if I bring my advocacy and openness, and they bring knowledge, emotional intelligence, and a genuine desire to support me, together we create something powerful. They remind me that allies don't have to be perfect, they just have to be willing.

In the groups I've facilitated with people working through *Becoming Hearing Empowered*, one of the deepest pains they share is that the people closest to them don't truly understand what they are going through. They describe the loneliness of bluffing through conversations, the sting of being dismissed with a "never mind," and the frustration of not being believed when they explain what they need. Again and again, I hear the same longing: *I just wish the people in my life could know what this feels like.*

That is why I've written this book: *Becoming an Empowered Hearing Ally*. While *Becoming Hearing Empowered* gives people with hearing loss a space to reflect and grow, very few resources exist for the people who stand beside them. This book is that resource, written just for you: a parent, a coworker, a partner, a friend. It will help you bridge the gap, build understanding, and give you the knowledge and tools to support your loved one with confidence and care.

That's what this book is about: learning how to become a more empowered ally.

A Word About Words

Many terms describe hearing loss: *deaf, hard of hearing, late-deafened, hearing disability, hearing impaired,* and more. Each word carries its own history, emotions, and meaning. Some people strongly prefer one label; others reject the same word as offensive or inaccurate.

For example, *hearing impaired* has been widely debated. Some dislike it because "impaired" implies weakness or damage. Others choose to use it and find it fits their experience. There is no single "right" answer. What matters most is respecting the language each individual chooses for themselves.

In this book, I use **hearing loss** as a broad umbrella term for clarity. You'll see different terms throughout, giving you the opportunity to become familiar with them and to consider how your loved one wants to describe their own experience.

You'll also notice **d/Deaf**. This spelling acknowledges both groups within the broader community. Lowercase "deaf" refers to people who describe their level of hearing loss, while uppercase "Deaf" refers to those who primarily use sign language, connect socially with the Deaf community, and share its rich cultural traditions. You'll learn more about this distinction in Chapter 5, for now, just know that both terms honor real identities.

One more note: while I frequently use *loved one* to describe the person with hearing loss in your life, the guidance in this book applies much more broadly. An **ally** is anyone who chooses to support a person with hearing loss with awareness, compassion, and responsibility, whether you're a friend, partner, child, coworker, teacher, supervisor, or occasional communication partner. Hearing loss affects relationships of all kinds, not just family ties. If you're a boss, colleague, teacher, or teammate, you play an equally important role in creating understanding and access. This book is for you, too.

Throughout, I'll also use *friend, person with hearing loss,* and *communication partner* to reflect this range.

You've decided to read and reflect through this book to learn more about hearing loss and how to become a stronger, more compassionate ally. This is an opportunity to consider how hearing loss affects your loved one, how it impacts your relationship, and how to support communication, identity, and self-care in ways that build connection instead of frustration.

Before you turn the page, sit with these questions:

- What moment made me pick up this book? What was I feeling?

- What do I most fear getting wrong?

- What would it mean, for me and for my loved one, if I got this right?

Let this be your starting point as you prepare to grow into the role of an empowered hearing ally.

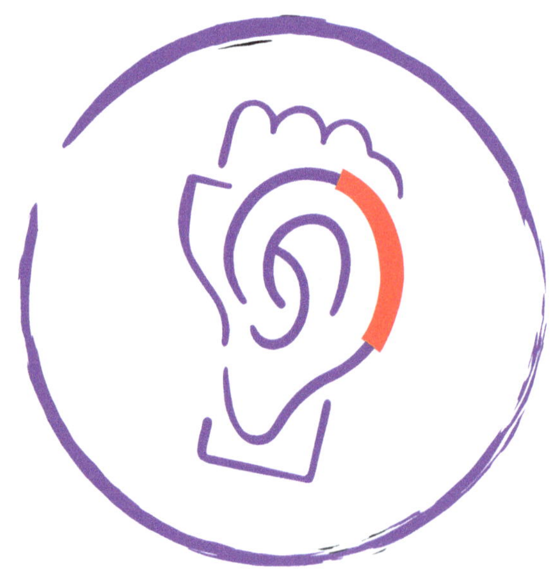

BECOMING AN EMPOWERED HEARING ALLY

2 | mindset

There was a restaurant we used to love. Great food, nice atmosphere, always packed. My brother and I met there for lunch every few weeks for years. But after his hearing loss progressed, we stopped going.

"It's too loud," I said. "You can't hear anything there."

He didn't argue. We just... stopped.

A year later, a friend mentioned the restaurant started offering a quiet back room on weeknights. I hadn't known. I hadn't asked. I'd just decided it was impossible and closed the door.

That's when I realized: I'd been making decisions based on what I assumed couldn't work, instead of asking what might. I'd given up on places, on traditions, on possibilities, without ever really considering other options.

I wondered how many other doors I'd closed without checking if they were actually locked.

Section 1: What is Mindset?

Mindset shapes how both you and your loved one approach the challenges of hearing loss. When you choose patience, openness, and encouragement, you not only support their growth, you strengthen your own role as an ally.

A key foundation to your communication partner's success in this whole process is their mindset. Everything they do, feel, and believe is profoundly influenced by the way they think. Mindset reframes beliefs about what they are capable of and opens new opportunities to discover empowerment. Researchers have discovered the power of mindset, and its principles are now applied in schools, businesses, relationships, and even parenting.

How do we think about our talents, our abilities, our disabilities, our skills? Does the way we think about these things change outcomes? How do these thoughts influence success in our jobs, our friendships, our families, and our favorite pastimes?

In this chapter, you will learn what mindset is, why it matters, the difference between fixed and growth mindsets, and how to nurture a growth mindset in your relationship.

What is Mindset?

Put simply, mindset is the attitude and the words we use to talk to ourselves when faced with a frustrating situation. A mindset is developed by reflecting on experiences; changing those thought patterns reshapes how someone views the world.

And because mindset is shaped by thinking, it is also changed through new ways of thinking.

Here's a glimpse into how mindset shows up in the life of someone with hearing loss:

Imagine your loved one is at a friend's house, ready to watch a movie. Their friend hasn't turned on the captions. After waiting a few minutes to see if their friend realizes they need the captions, the friend instead continues watching the movie and munching popcorn. Your loved one feels invisible or frustrated. This moment brings up other memories of times when they've felt excluded: missing a work announcement, not catching a joke, or feeling lost in a group conversation. Tonight is the last straw.

Thoughts and feelings are fueled and validated by their current mindset, and what happens next depends on their mindset:

- They grab the remote, turn captions on with annoyance, and stew about how often they're overlooked.

- They snap and leave, deciding it isn't worth staying.

- They pause the movie and tell their friend they are struggling and feel hurt, opening the door to connection.

Only one of these options feeds a sense of empowerment and supports your friend's positive self-esteem. But that option, pausing the movie and talking about their feelings, often feels like the hardest choice. When someone tells themselves, "What's the point? This will just happen again tomorrow," they fall into discouragement.

This is why mindset matters. Mindset profoundly affects the way we live our life, and for someone with a hearing loss, it impacts their ability to connect with others, to thrive socially, professionally, and personally. A fixed mindset fuels frustration and resignation, while a growth mindset makes room for self-esteem, resilience, and advocacy.

We can reframe our lives with a different mindset. We can find opportunity after opportunity to grow and become who we've always wanted to be, because of, and in spite of, a hearing loss, our childhood, or past difficult relationships. We can persevere in the face of adversity. We can expand and develop and change and adapt. We can discover our inner strength, build self-esteem, and develop empowering advocacy and ally skills that improve our relationships and move us forward on a new path. This is 100% possible for you, for your friend with hearing loss, for all of us.

This is the power of mindset.

The right mindset fuels opportunities to move from frustration and limitation toward resilience and empowerment. And as their ally, understanding this shift helps you recognize just how central mindset is in shaping your loved one's confidence and quality of life.

ALLY IN ACTION

Begin applying this idea right away by:

- **Observing:** Pay attention to when your communication partner seems discouraged or energized in communication. This often reflects a negative or positive mindset at work.

- **Asking:** Instead of assuming what they're thinking, ask: "That situation seemed really frustrating. Do you want to share some of the thoughts you had when it happened?"

- **Modeling:** Share an example when you recognized negative thoughts about a situation and you now see that those thoughts likely influenced how you felt.

ALLY INSIGHTS

- When I notice my friend getting discouraged, do I usually step in, stay quiet, or change the subject? How might my response influence their mindset?

- Have I assumed their reaction was "overly sensitive" without considering how often they face these barriers?

- What is one small change to make this week to show my friend that I believe in their ability to grow and adapt?

Section 2: Fixed vs. Growth Mindset

ALLY PERSPECTIVE: WHY THIS MATTERS

A fixed mindset, whether yours or your loved one's, makes hearing loss feel like a permanent barrier. A growth mindset opens the door to adaptation, problem-solving, and stronger relationships. By choosing growth yourself, you model resilience and make it easier for your loved one to do the same.

Fixed Mindset

A fixed mindset is the belief that who we are, our abilities, and our role in life are already predetermined. It feels like we are stuck with the cards we've been dealt: our place of birth, our family background, past experiences, our education, and more. From this perspective, changing our path feels nearly impossible.

A fixed mindset for someone with hearing loss focuses on their diagnosis: the severity of their hearing loss, whether it is progressive or stable, and how well technology is, or isn't, working for them.

They find themselves constantly trying to prove they are "enough": smart enough, capable enough, hearing enough, or even deaf enough. With this mindset, they accept the belief that because of their hearing loss, they will always miss out on important parts of life: friendships, social events, relationships, jobs, jokes, conversations, and connections. The conclusion becomes: there's not much I can do about it.

A fixed mindset also influences relationships. Someone who feels stuck believes that the way they communicate with their partner, parent, child, friend, or sibling is "just how it is" and cannot be improved. They assume the other person's habits, communication style, or empathy level will never really change. Even if some pieces of the relationship feel painful or unsatisfying, the fixed mindset suggests nothing will make it better.

People caught in this mindset are more likely to give up in the face of challenges because they believe they're permanently stuck. Their inner dialogue focuses on judgment and avoiding mistakes, rather than growth and problem-solving.

Growth Mindset

A growth mindset, on the other hand, is the belief that who we are, our abilities, and even our relationships can change and improve. With effort, new strategies, and support from others, our life path is not fixed but open to new possibilities.

Yes, your friend with hearing loss was dealt a certain set of circumstances, but those circumstances don't define their ultimate potential. Hearing loss, family history, and past struggles become the starting point, not the endpoint, on the road to empowerment. Their true potential is unknown and cannot be predicted; it grows as they learn, practice, and adapt with support and resilience.

A growth mindset also changes relationships. With this perspective, communication and connection are seen as fluid and adaptable. Just because something feels hard now doesn't mean it will always feel that way. You and your friend don't yet fully understand how to communicate effectively with hearing loss, but you will grow and learn. Together, you will develop new ways of relating, talking, and supporting one another.

When setbacks happen, people with a growth mindset are more likely to persevere. Rather than shutting down, they view challenges as opportunities to adapt. Their internal dialogue shifts from judgment to learning, from hopelessness to constructive action.

The key for your loved one is moving away from hiding, pretending, or silently nodding along. Instead, a growth mindset means embracing hearing loss as part of who they are, advocating openly, and finding out just how much is possible when they give themselves permission to grow.

Find out what you can accomplish together when you both believe that you can develop new skills and strategies. This is an opportunity for both of you to allow yourselves the time and the space to become more empowered.

Your Growth vs. Fixed Mindset

The mindset of a person with hearing loss is central to how they see themselves, but your mindset as their ally matters too.

Your fixed mindset sounds like:

- "They'll never be able to follow along in noisy places, so we just can't do things like that anymore."

- "I'll never remember to change how I speak. I always forget and end up mumbling or turning away mid-sentence."

- "We'll never be able to enjoy concerts together; it's just not possible."

- "A voice phone call isn't an option for us; we'll just always have to text."

A growth mindset reframes those same situations into possibilities:

- "Crowded restaurants are tough, but if I suggest a quieter place or explore assistive tech, we'll both enjoy ourselves more."

- "I still forget to face them or slow down, but I'm getting better with practice and by asking them to gently remind me."

- "Concerts are loud and challenging, but we're looking into venues with good captioning, quieter outdoor performances, or assistive listening devices so we can still share the experience."

- "Phone calls are tough, but captioned phone services or apps make them manageable when we really need to talk that way."

Practicing a growth mindset means believing that communication challenges are not dead ends, but opportunities to adapt, communicate with, and support your friend with hearing loss. It means shifting from blame or frustration to curiosity and problem-solving. When you assume growth is possible, you help remove invisible weight they've been carrying.

ALLY IN ACTION

Here are a few ways to apply a growth mindset starting today:

- **Tonight at dinner**, before speaking, get their attention and wait for eye contact, then notice if you feel impatient.

- **This week**, when communication breaks down, say out loud: "We haven't figured this out yet" instead of sighing or going silent.

- **When they try something new**, a new app, a new way of asking for repeats, a new seating arrangement, respond with "I noticed you tried that. How did it feel?" rather than evaluating whether it "worked."

ALLY INSIGHTS

- When communication fails repeatedly, what's the first thought that crosses my mind? Is it about them ("They're not trying") or the situation ("We need a different approach")?

- Have I ever thought, or said, "This is just how it's going to be"? What was I protecting myself from by believing that?

In *Becoming Hearing Empowered*, your loved one works on an activity called **What Mindset Do I Have?** They circle statements that resonate with them, then revisit those statements to see whether they reflect a fixed mindset or a growth mindset.

If your loved one is working on this activity, you might ask: "Would you like to share a statement that surprised you?"

Wait for them to lead. If most of what they found leans toward a fixed mindset, resist the urge to reassure or fix, simply say, "Thank you for showing me that." Recognizing patterns is the first step toward growth, and your calm acceptance makes it safer for them to be honest about where they are.

Section 3: Changing Your Mindset

A growth mindset gives both you and your loved one another way to be. When you slip into a fixed mindset, it feels like communication challenges will never change. Choosing growth reminds you that effort, creativity, and "not yet" lead to new strategies and deeper connection with your loved one.

Fixed Mindset in Hearing Loss

A fixed mindset pressures a person with hearing loss to avoid challenges, such as participating in a group discussion that exposes the fact that they don't hear as well as others. The instinct is to hide, nod, or withdraw. A growth mindset reframes that same challenge as a chance to educate others, use a captioning app, or use an assistive listening device to improve access.

A fixed mindset urges them not to bother learning sign language, not to explore a new assistive device, or not to keep working through these strategies. "It won't make any difference. It's a waste of time." A growth mindset instead applauds every attempt at learning new ways to communicate and self-advocate. Over time, those efforts build empowerment and self-esteem.

Your Fixed Mindset

A fixed mindset also shows up for you. You might think:

- "I'll never be able to understand what they need from me."

- "There's no point inviting them to group dinners; they'll just feel left out."

- "I shouldn't speak up about captions or accessibility at work; it's not my place."

- "My coworker probably doesn't want me to repeat things; it will embarrass them."

With a growth mindset, however, you can see these challenges as opportunities:

- "I don't have to know everything right away; I'll ask, listen, and learn from my friend."

- "I'll suggest smaller gatherings or turn off background noise, so they stay included."

- "Speaking up about captions helps everyone, not just my communication partner."

- "I'll quietly check in and ask how to support them instead of assuming what's best."

Remember: Change Takes Time

Changing mindset isn't like flipping a switch. Even with a growth mindset, your inner voice (and your loved one's) will still slip into old judgments: hiding hearing aids, nodding to cover up not understanding, or becoming irritable when captions aren't turned on.

A growth mindset doesn't erase those moments; it simply shines a light on them. It gives both of you another chance to grow, show grace, and re-engage with curiosity and empowerment.

Strategies to Help Shift Toward Growth

- Embrace the Process. Growth isn't about perfection, it's about the ongoing work of learning, reflecting, and trying again. For you, that means practicing communication strategies and being patient when you forget. For your friend with hearing loss, it means seeing each advocacy attempt as a success, no matter the outcome.

- Embrace the Power of "Yet." Reframe discouraging thoughts with "yet." Instead of: "We don't enjoy dinner parties together." Say: "We haven't figured out how to enjoy dinner parties yet." This small word opens the door to creative solutions: trying remote microphones, requesting captions, or adjusting seating to improve inclusion.

- Pay Attention to Self-Talk. Mindset is shaped by the language we use with ourselves. Notice if your self-talk is judgmental: "I'm terrible at this." Reframe it: "I'm still learning how to do this well." Encourage your loved one to do the same but also model it yourself. You are both learners in this process.

- **Say it out loud:** The next time you forget to face them or speak clearly, say "I'm still learning" instead of "Sorry, sorry."

- **Before a challenging outing**, a restaurant, family gathering, or work event, ask: "What's one thing I can do to make this easier for you?"

- **After a hard moment**, resist the urge to analyze what went wrong. Instead, simply say: "That was tough. Want to try again tomorrow?"

- Complete this sentence honestly: "I've stopped trying to ___________ because I don't think it will ever work."

- Now add "yet" to the end. How does that change what feels possible?

In *Becoming Hearing Empowered*, your loved one is working on the activity **Reframing**, where they take fixed mindset thoughts they identified earlier and rewrite them into growth mindset statements. For example:

Fixed: "With my hearing loss, I just can't function at a dinner party."

Growth: "I haven't figured out how to enjoy myself at a dinner party yet."

If your loved one shares a reframed statement, try responding with: "What made you choose that new way of thinking?"

Listen without correcting or improving their answer. If it feels right, offer one of your own: "I've been trying to reframe _____." Showing that you're doing this work makes the process feel shared rather than one-sided.

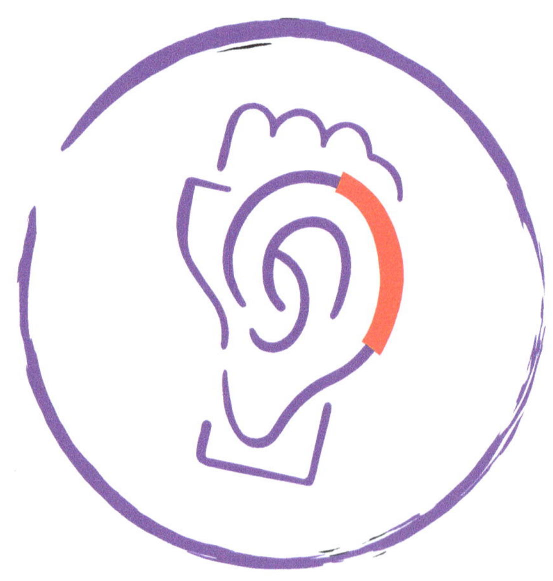

3 | hearing loss 101

The audiologist pointed to the graph and said something about "sloping to severe in the high frequencies." My wife nodded. I nodded too, but I had no idea what I was nodding at.

The lines on the paper meant nothing to me. I didn't know which direction was "worse." I didn't understand why some sounds mattered more than others. I couldn't connect any of it to the moments at home when she'd miss the doorbell or ask me to repeat the ends of my sentences.

I wanted to ask questions, but I didn't even know what to ask.

That's when I realized: if I was going to support her, I needed to understand what I was looking at.

Section 1: Ear Anatomy

ALLY PERSPECTIVE: WHY THIS MATTERS

Knowing how the ear works helps you move beyond thinking of hearing loss as just "quiet" or "loud." It gives you a clearer picture of what your loved one is experiencing, and it also helps you feel more prepared when medical or technology decisions, like hearing aids or implants, are discussed.

In this chapter, you'll learn the basic science of hearing loss. Understanding how the ear works, how sound is processed, and which parts of the ear are not functioning properly will help you support your communication partner more effectively.

Hearing loss isn't simply "everything is quieter." Depending on which part of the ear is affected, it changes the way your friend hears sound or understands speech in their daily life. By learning how to read an audiogram and describe hearing loss accurately, you'll gain a clearer picture of what communication challenges they face.

This knowledge equips you to be a better partner in conversations about treatment, technology, changes in hearing over time, and accommodations. It also gives you the confidence to ask thoughtful questions and recognize when a strategy is, or isn't, working for your loved one.

Labeled Diagram of the Ear Anatomy

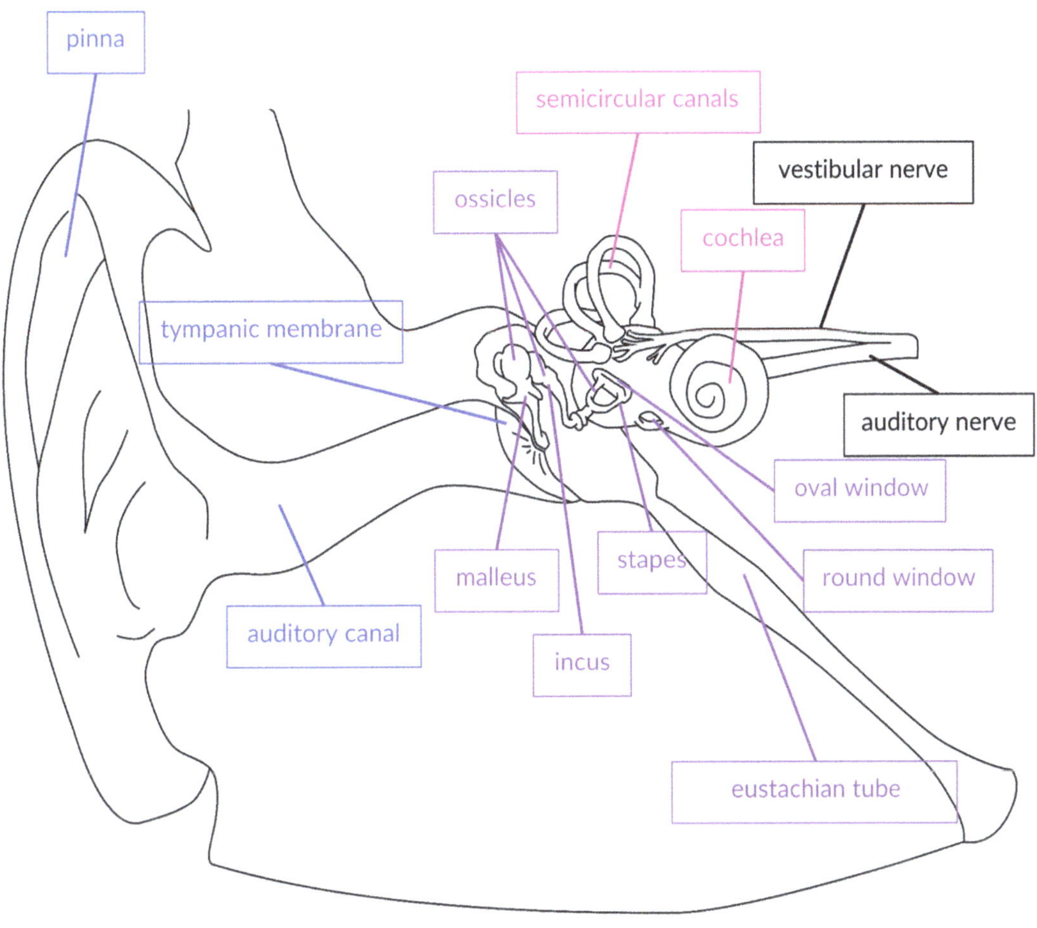

Diagram created by Kaitlin Walsh of Lyon Road Art

Ear Anatomy

Ear anatomy is divided into three main areas:

- Outer ear: includes the pinna (the visible part), the auditory canal, and the tympanic membrane (eardrum).

- Middle ear: contains three tiny bones called ossicles (malleus/hammer, incus/anvil, stapes/stirrup), as well as the oval window, round window, and eustachian tube. The middle ear should normally be a dry, air-filled space.

- Inner ear: includes the cochlea and semicircular canals. The auditory nerve connects to the cochlea and carries electrical sound signals to the brain. The vestibular nerve connects to the semicircular canals and carries balance signals. Because of this connection, dizziness or vertigo occurs with certain types of hearing loss. Both the cochlea and semicircular canals are fluid-filled and lined with tiny receptors, called stereocilia, that create electrical signals for the brain.

Understanding these parts is the first step to recognizing how hearing loss develops and how it affects everyday communication.

Check out **hearingoutloud.net/resources** for helpful links and more information

- **Connect anatomy with experience.** When your friend explains their hearing loss, link what they describe to the parts of the ear you've learned about. It helps you understand why certain situations are harder than others. (For example, if your friend hears sound but not words clearly, damage in the cochlea can make speech sound distorted.)

- **Ask informed questions.** Use this knowledge at appointments or when discussing accommodations to better support their needs.

- **Look beyond volume.** Remember that hearing loss often involves clarity, distortion, or balance, not just how loud something is.

- Before today, how did I picture hearing loss? Did I think of it only as "quiet" or "loud"?

- How does knowing about the outer, middle, and inner ear help me better understand what my communication partner experiences?

- How might I use this knowledge during their medical appointments?

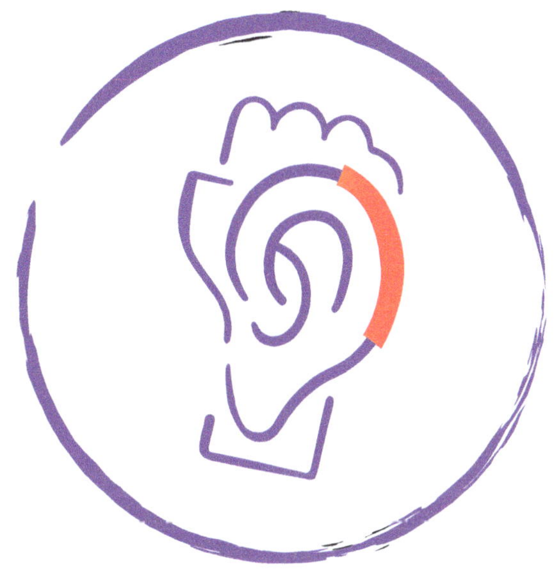

In *Becoming Hearing Empowered,* your loved one's journal activity is **Diagram of the Ear**. You can do the same activity here. This shared activity helps reinforce what you've both learned, and it creates a common language you can use when talking about hearing loss. Label the diagram below with the following parts, and if you like, add color or decoration:

outer ear, middle ear, inner ear, pinna, ear canal, tympanic membrane (eardrum), ossicles (malleus,, incus, stapes), eustachian tube, cochlea, oval window, round window, auditory nerve, semicircular canals, vestibular nerve

Section 2: The Process of Hearing & Types of Hearing Loss

ALLY PERSPECTIVE: WHY THIS MATTERS

Learning how sound travels through air and bone gives you context for why different types of hearing loss need different solutions. This understanding helps you follow conversations about audiograms, treatment options, and devices like hearing aids or bone-anchored implants with more confidence.

The Process of Hearing

The process of hearing is incredibly complex. We receive sound in two ways: through **air conduction** and **bone conduction**. Understanding both will be important when we talk about audiograms in upcoming sections. If you're a visual learner, search YouTube for videos illustrating the process of hearing.

Air Conduction

In **air conduction**, what begins as a sound pressure wave funneled in by the outer ear becomes mechanical energy as it moves through the bones in the middle ear, converts to hydraulic energy inside the cochlea of the inner ear, and is finally converted to electrical energy and is sent through the auditory nerve to the brain.

The **pinna** acts like a funnel, capturing sound waves and sending them through the **auditory canal**. When the sound waves reach the **tympanic membrane**, it vibrates like a drum. The vibration moves the **ossicles** in the middle ear: first the **malleus**, then the **incus**, and finally the **stapes**. The stapes pushes against the **oval window**, creating tiny waves in the liquid of the **cochlea**, while the **round window** bulges outward in response to the pressure.

Inside the cochlea, tiny hair cells called **stereocilia** move in response to the waves, much like seaweed swaying in the ocean. The cochlea itself is a small, snail-shaped coil, and the stereocilia are arranged along it like piano keys, from high to low pitch.

High-pitched sounds stimulate stereocilia at the base of the cochlea.

Low-pitched sounds travel farther along the coil before being detected.

When the stereocilia move, they convert the hydraulic energy into electrical signals, which the **auditory nerve** then carries to the brain. Our brain interprets these signals as sound. This entire sequence is known as **air conduction**.

Bone Conduction

There is another way we perceive sound, called **bone conduction**. This occurs when the **bones of the skull** (not the middle ear bones) vibrate, directly stimulating the fluid inside the **cochlea**. Bone conduction does not rely on the outer or middle ear. You've likely experienced this with bone conduction headphones, which rest next to the ears rather than over them, or heard of bone anchored hearing aids (BAHA) that send vibrations straight to the cochlea. These vibrations activate the same **stereocilia** that send electrical sound signals to the brain.

When you think about the vast diversity of sounds our mouths create to form words, and imagine each sound transmitted through this intricate system, it's amazing how sensitive hearing must be to distinguish between words like "lake" and "like" or "tart" and "start."

Other Important Structures in the Ear

Other structures in the ear do not participate directly in the process of hearing, but they play important roles as well.

The **eustachian tube**, which connects the middle ear to the throat, equalizes air pressure and prevents fluid buildup in the middle ear. This allows air conduction to occur more easily. You've likely experienced an ear infection or a "head cold" where your ears felt full and it was more difficult to hear. You've probably also felt your ears "pop" when changing altitude in a plane or car created a difference in air pressure. The eustachian tube is responsible for draining fluid when you're sick, and releasing or increasing the air pressure of the middle ear when there is a difference in air pressure around you.

Babies get middle ear infections more easily than adults because their eustachian tubes are shorter and more horizontal, allowing fluid and germs to become trapped. Tubes are often placed in the eardrum to allow fluid to drain until the child's eustachian tubes grow longer and more vertical.

The **vestibular system** (connected to the cochlea) consists of the semicircular canals and the vestibular nerve. They provide the brain with information about motion, head position, and spatial orientation. The semicircular canals and cochlea share the same inner ear fluid (endolymph). Some people with hearing loss have Meniere's disease, which is caused by abnormal amounts of this fluid. It results in both hearing loss and vertigo (dizziness).

Types of Hearing Loss

There are three main types of hearing loss: **conductive**, **sensorineural**, and **mixed**.

Conductive Hearing Loss occurs when sound waves do not get through the outer and/or middle ear. Differences in the shape of the pinna or auditory canal, a ruptured eardrum, fluid in the middle ear, or problems with the ossicles, all interfere with sound waves reaching the cochlea. Causes include frequent ear infections, earwax buildup, perforated eardrum, benign tumors, and otosclerosis (abnormal bone growth in the middle ear). Surgery improves conductive hearing loss in some cases.

Sensorineural Hearing Loss (SNHL) occurs when the inner ear (cochlea, stereocilia, or auditory nerve) is not functioning properly. Imagine the tiny hair cells in the cochlea like seaweed, swaying in the ocean as the waves roll over it. The stereocilia become damaged, bent, or broken and no longer activate electrical signals. Remember the stereocilia are arranged along the entire coil of the cochlea. Those that are at the base of the coil are responsible for high pitched sounds, and those toward the center of the coil respond to low pitched sounds. High-frequency hearing loss typically results from damage to the stereocilia at the base of the cochlea. In this case, the person with hearing loss has difficulty hearing high pitched sounds, but middle and low sounds are perceived more easily.

One of the most common causes of sensorineural hearing loss is damage to the stereocilia from loud noise. Other causes of sensorineural hearing loss include illness, ototoxic medications, genetics, and the natural aging process. Most of the time, medicine or surgery cannot restore this type of hearing.

Mixed Hearing Loss is a combination of both conductive and sensorineural hearing loss.

Noise and Trauma-Induced Hearing Loss

Listening to loud music or being exposed to loud machinery permanently damages the stereocilia in the cochlea. Very loud, sudden noises (like gunshots or explosions) break them instantly. Repeated exposure (like loud concerts or headphones turned up high) wears them out over time. In addition, violent shaking (such as concussion) or blows to the head also can damage stereocilia. This damage is irreversible. Protecting ears with earplugs or earmuffs, turning down the volume, taking breaks from loud environments, and protecting your head from trauma are all ways to prevent further loss.

Tinnitus

Tinnitus (TIN-ni-tus or tin-NYE-tus) is ringing, buzzing, roaring, hissing, clicking, or humming heard in one or both ears without an external sound source. It frequently accompanies sensorineural hearing loss because damaged stereocilia "leak" random electrical impulses. Other causes include ear infections, Meniere's disease, eustachian tube dysfunction, otosclerosis, and inner ear muscle spasms. Tinnitus ranges from mild to severe, and in many cases causes stress, sleep issues, concentration difficulties, depression, or anxiety. Hearing aids frequently help, and treatment options should be discussed with an audiologist or ENT (Ear, Nose and Throat) doctor, also called an otolaryngologist.

ALLY IN ACTION

- **Recognize the differences.** Not all hearing loss is the same. Some comes from outer or middle ear issues (conductive), while others involve the inner ear or auditory nerve (sensorineural).

- **Protect hearing together.** Be mindful of noise exposure, which can cause permanent damage. Use ear protection or avoid loud environments when possible. Use helmets during sports and recreation, and take steps to prevent falls and concussions in everyday life.

- **Respond with patience.** Tinnitus can be exhausting and stressful. If your friend with hearing loss mentions "ringing" or seems distracted, offer understanding and support.

- Had I thought of hearing loss as just "turning down the volume"? How does this new knowledge expand my perspective?

- What can I do to help reduce noise exposure for myself and my friend with hearing loss?

- How can I show empathy when my communication partner describes tinnitus or balance issues?

In *Becoming Hearing Empowered*, your loved one is completing an activity called **Locations of Hearing Loss**. You can do this alongside them. Use your art supplies to indicate the locations of each type of hearing loss on the diagram:

- Conductive Hearing Loss

- Sensorineural Hearing Loss

This shared activity helps both of you visualize the difference between the types of hearing loss and makes it easier to discuss them together.

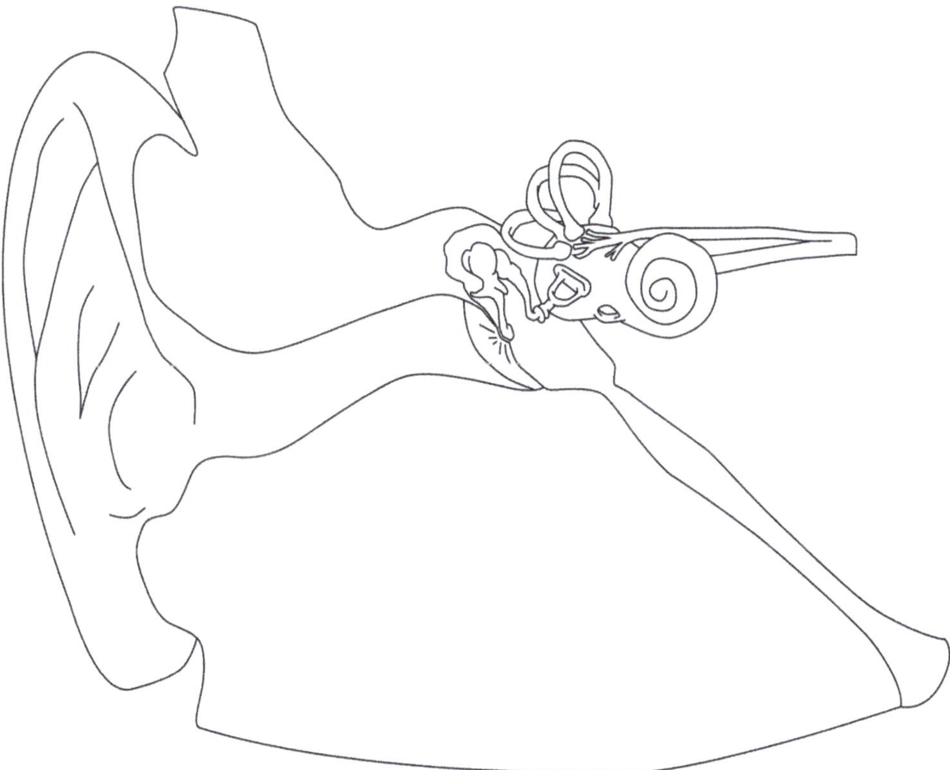

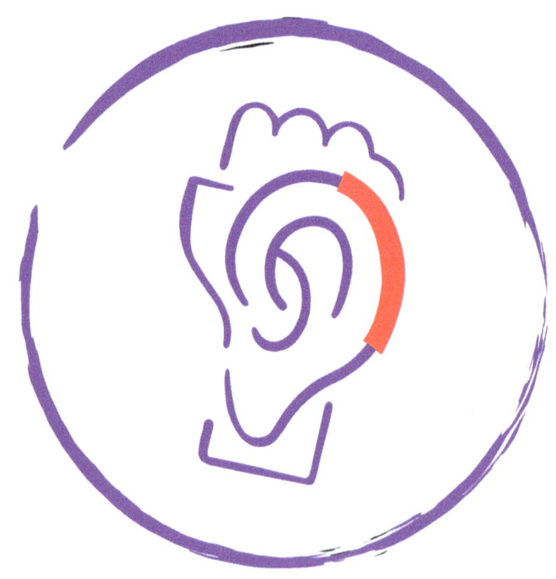

BECOMING AN EMPOWERED HEARING ALLY

Section 3: Hearing Testing (Part 1)

ALLY PERSPECTIVE: WHY THIS MATTERS

An audiogram (a graph that records the results of a hearing test) is a valuable tool, but it only reflects hearing in quiet, ideal conditions. Knowing both what it shows and what it leaves out helps you understand why your friend with hearing loss still struggles in noisy environments, and it prepares you to ask better questions and make informed choices about hearing aids, implants, or other technology.

When someone is given a hearing test, the audiologist will likely bring them into a soundproof booth. They will go through a variety of tests and be asked to respond when they hear tones, beeps, and words played into the left or right ear. An audiogram is a graph, along with other tables and text, showing the results of the hearing test. Because the test is done in a soundproof booth, most of the results represent what a person hears in a perfect listening environment.

Keep in mind: even though the audiogram tells you about the speech sounds that are most difficult for someone to hear, it does not show how well they will comprehend speech in noisy, everyday environments. The audiogram does not account for the cognitive effects experienced by d/Deaf and Hard of Hearing people due to listening fatigue.

For someone with hearing loss, many factors contribute to how much they understand speech at any given moment: proximity to the speaker, prior knowledge of the topic, ability to focus, amount and type of background noise, cognitive energy spent filling in the blanks, current functioning of hearing devices and assistive technology, and the list goes on.

We'll explore these areas in upcoming chapters. For now, let's focus on what information an audiogram does provide.

Pure Tone Audiometry

The primary piece of information on an audiogram report is the graph where hearing thresholds are plotted. This graph consists of an x-axis and y-axis.

The **x-axis** (horizontal) represents frequency, measured in Hertz. Frequency indicates the pitch of a sound, ranging from low sounds on the left to high sounds on the right.

The **y-axis** (vertical) represents hearing level, measured in decibels. Hearing level indicates the loudness or intensity of a sound, ranging from very quiet at the top to very loud at the bottom.

When the audiologist plays a tone at a specific frequency (pitch), they place a mark at the line corresponding to the hearing level where the person just barely heard it. This is called their **hearing threshold**. This testing process is known as **pure tone audiometry**.

The Speech Banana

When the sounds of speech are plotted on the audiogram graph, the shape formed looks a bit like a banana, hence the name "speech banana." The purpose of the speech banana is to help make sense of the audiogram.

Remember: the marks on the graph are made when the sound is just barely heard, and in a near-perfect (silent) environment. The speech sounds located at these frequencies and decibel levels represent the approximate loudness of someone talking in a quiet environment, standing 2–3 feet away.

In real life, background noise and distance make listening more difficult. In those situations, the sounds of speech must be louder to be heard, so the speech banana would effectively move lower on the y-axis of the audiogram graph.

Audiogram Graph

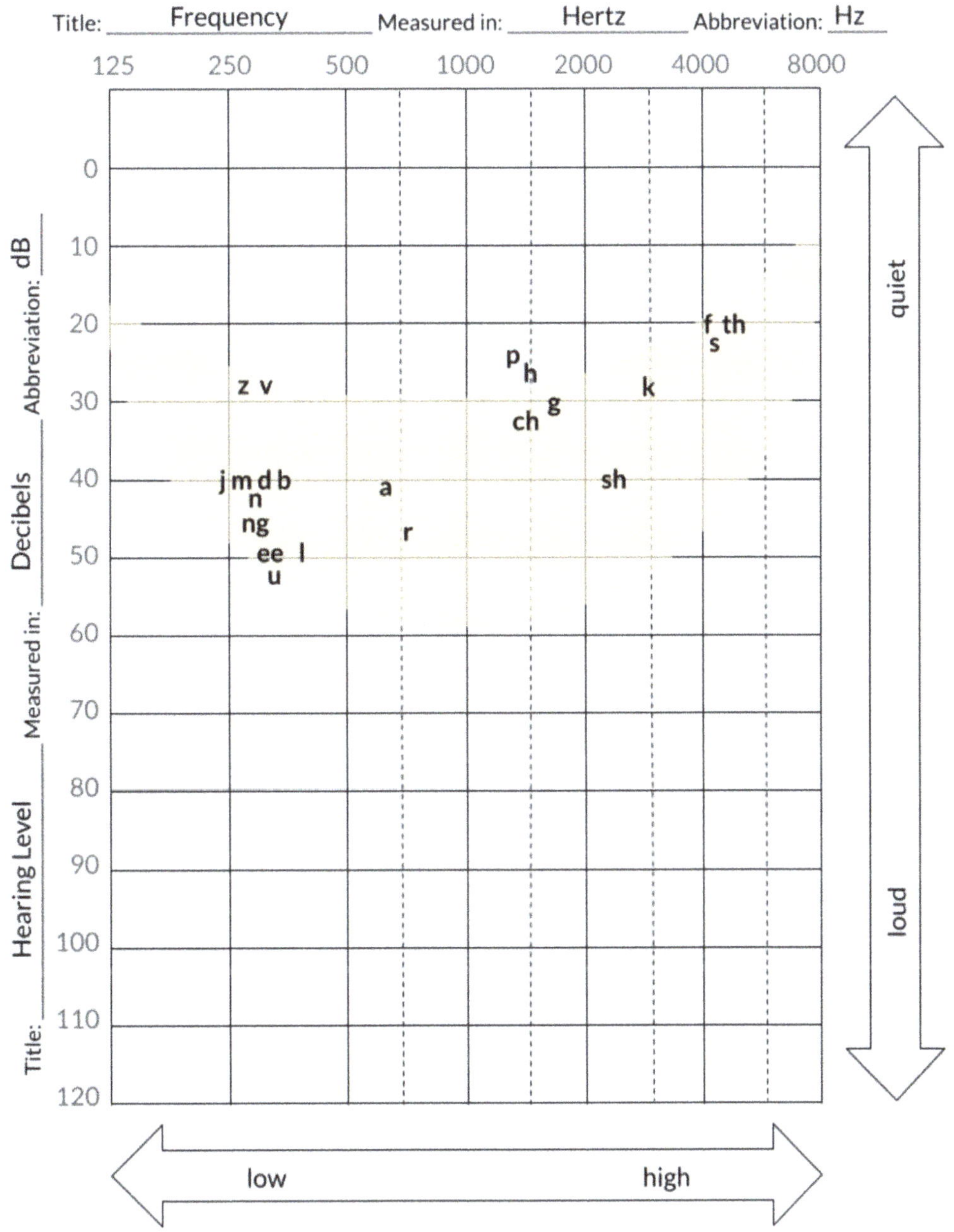

- **At their next audiology appointment**, ask the audiologist: "What does this audiogram not tell us about their daily experience?"

- **In a noisy restaurant this week**, mentally note: "This is what the audiogram can't measure." Let that awareness shape your patience.

- **If they share their audiogram, ask:** "What sounds or word endings give you the most trouble?" Their answer will tell you more than the graph alone.

ALLY INSIGHTS

- Before reading this section, what did I believe an audiogram measured? Where did that belief come from?

- Have I ever felt frustrated that their hearing "should be fine" based on test results? What was I not understanding?

In *Becoming Hearing Empowered*, your loved one completes an activity called **Audiogram Graph—Labeling**. They label the axes, mark "low to high" and "loud to soft," and place speech sounds on the graph.

You can do the same activity on the blank audiogram provided in this section. Doing it side by side, even if not at the same time, gives you a common reference point. The next time they mention struggling with certain sounds, you'll be able to picture exactly where those sounds fall on the graph.

If you complete this activity, consider asking them: "What parts of words or conversations does your audiogram help explain?" This turns a technical diagram into a conversation about their real experience.

Audiogram Graph: Labeling

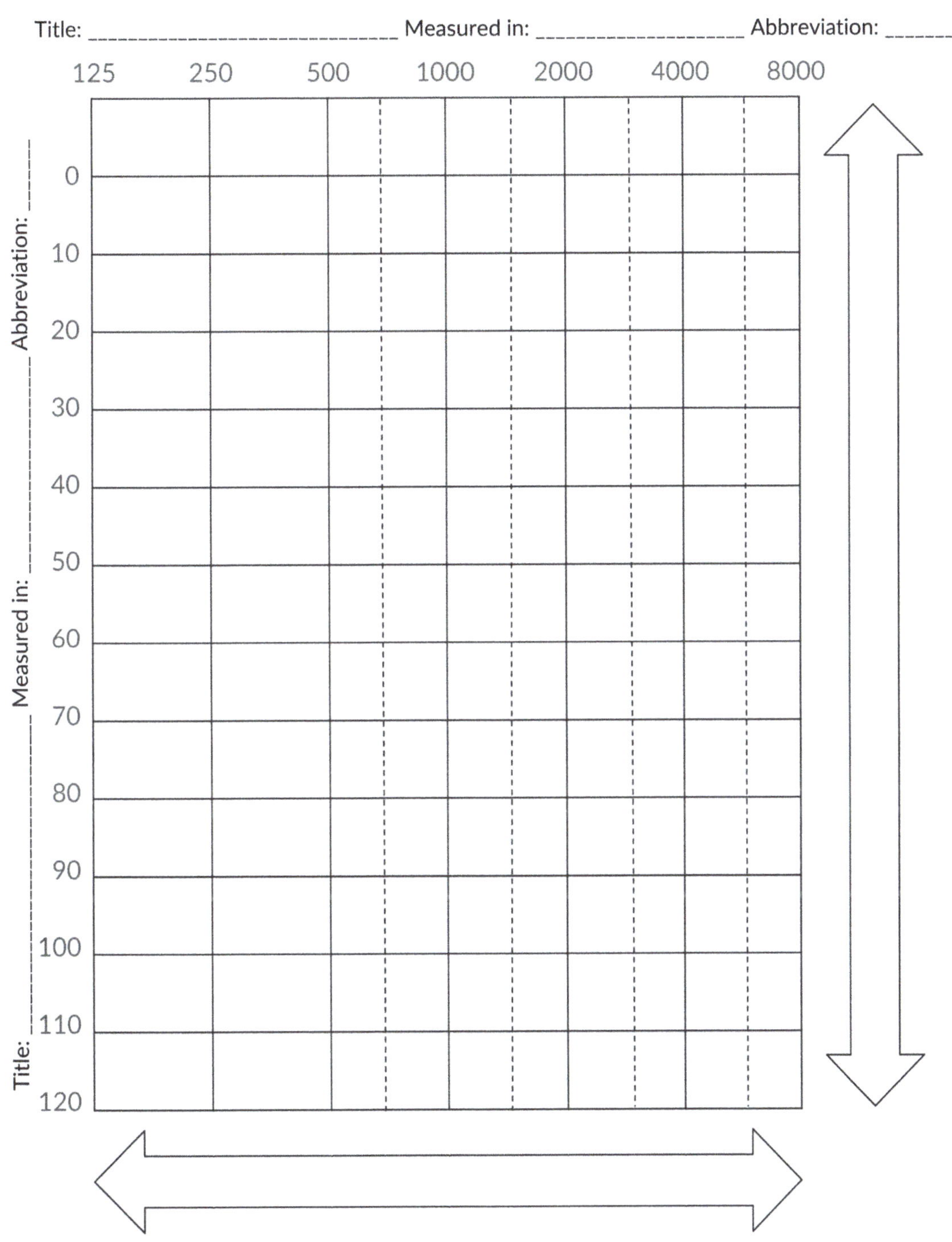

Section 4: Hearing Testing (Part 2)

Knowing the difference between air and bone conduction testing helps you understand how audiologists pinpoint the type of hearing loss. This insight makes it easier to follow your loved one's test results and support them in conversations about diagnosis and treatment.

Air Conduction Testing

Air conduction testing evaluates conductive hearing. The person being tested wears headphones or earphones for a portion of the test. During this time, the audiologist measures hearing through air conduction. Air conduction means the sounds are played into the ear and travel through the ear canal, vibrating the eardrum, causing the ossicles to vibrate. This in turn creates waves in the fluid in the cochlea, sending electrical signals to the auditory nerve, and finally to the brain, where these signals are perceived as sound.

Bone Conduction Testing

Bone conduction testing evaluates the inner ear, or sensorineural hearing. The audiologist places a tight headband (or bone conductor) over the head with a piece that sits on the mastoid bone, located behind the ear. This device delivers sound vibrations directly to the cochlea, bypassing the outer and middle ear entirely. This allows the audiologist to test the hearing sensitivity of the inner ear alone.

Masking

Masking is when one ear's cochlea is disengaged, or "kept busy," with white noise so that the other ear's bone conduction is tested more easily. When testing, the headphones, ear inserts, or bone conductor placed on the mastoid bone behind one ear vibrate the bones in the skull. Because this vibration is picked up by both cochleas, the audiologist plays white noise in one ear while testing the hearing in the other ear. The purpose of this is to keep the cochlea in the non-testing ear busy with noise, so when the person responds that they heard a beep, tone, or word, it is likely because they heard it in the ear being tested.

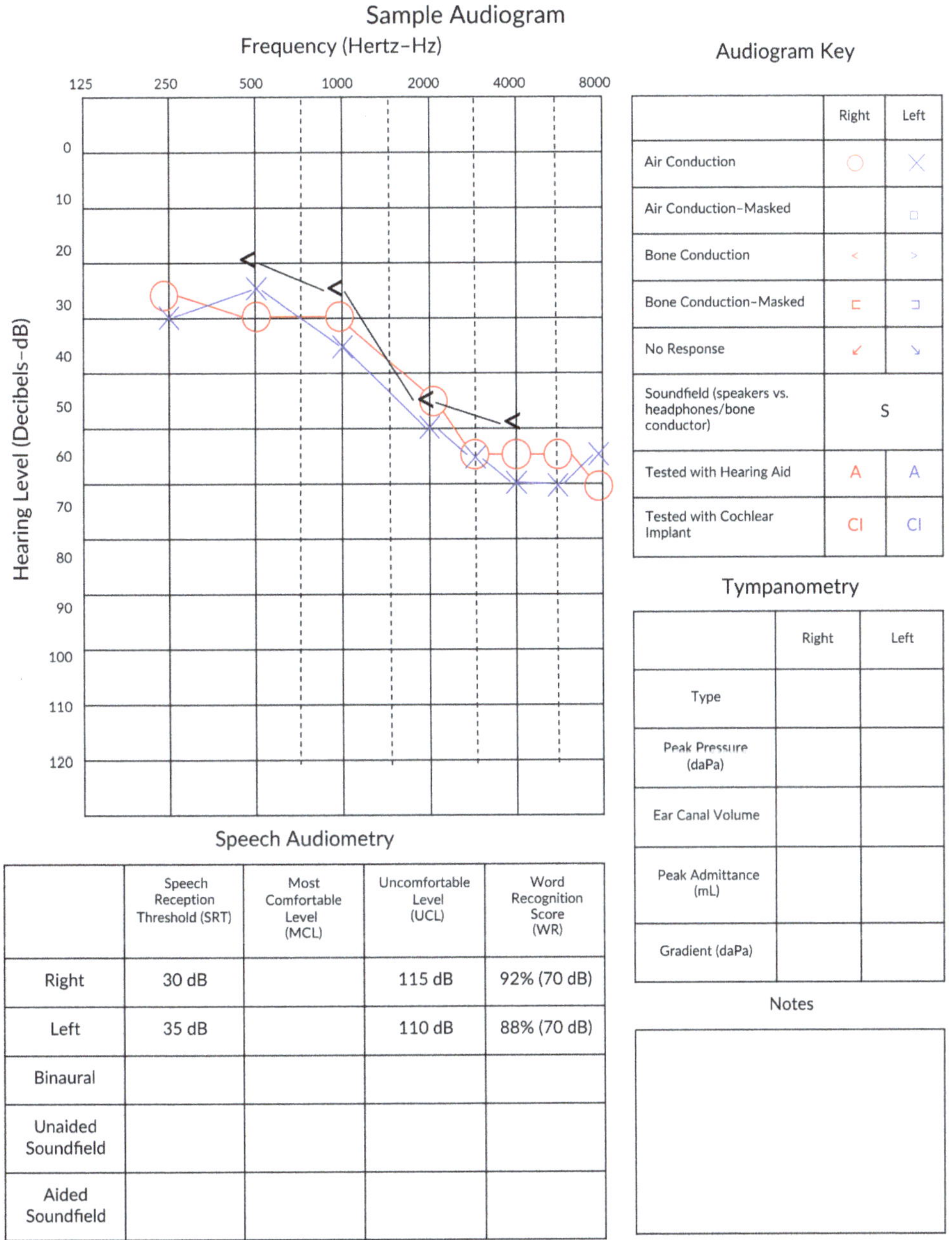

Audiogram Key

	Right	Left
Air Conduction	○	✕
Air Conduction–Masked		□
Bone Conduction	<	>
Bone Conduction–Masked	⊏	⊐
No Response	↙	↘
Soundfield (speakers vs. headphones/bone conductor)		S
Tested with Hearing Aid	A	A
Tested with Cochlear Implant	CI	CI

Tympanometry

	Right	Left
Type		
Peak Pressure (daPa)		
Ear Canal Volume		
Peak Admittance (mL)		
Gradient (daPa)		

Speech Audiometry

	Speech Reception Threshold (SRT)	Most Comfortable Level (MCL)	Uncomfortable Level (UCL)	Word Recognition Score (WR)
Right	30 dB		115 dB	92% (70 dB)
Left	35 dB		110 dB	88% (70 dB)
Binaural				
Unaided Soundfield				
Aided Soundfield				

Notes

Marking Symbols

Audiologists use different symbols of varied shape and color to convey hearing test results. An audiogram symbol key is provided for reference.

Air conduction testing, using headphones or ear inserts, is marked with four symbols: Unmasked: red circle (right ear) and blue x (left ear). When using masking: red triangle and blue square.

Bone conduction testing, using the bone conductor placed behind the ear, is marked with four symbols: Unmasked: red < and blue >. When using masking: red [and blue].

Symbols with a downward arrow indicate that the person did not hear the sound.

Less common symbols include: **S**: sound presented using speakers in the booth rather than headphones or inserts. **A** or **CI**: testing done while wearing a hearing aid (A) or cochlear implant (CI).

When reading an audiogram, keep in mind that for each frequency, any decibel levels above the mark were inaudible during the test.

Audiogram Key

	Right	Left
Air Conduction	O	X
Air Conduction-Masked	△	☐
Bone Conduction	<	>
Bone Conduction-Masked	⊏	⊐
No Response	↙	↘
Soundfield (speakers vs. headphones/bone conductor)	S	
Tested with Hearing Aid	A	A
Tested with Cochlear Implant	CI	CI

- **Learn the symbols.** Familiarize yourself with the basic audiogram symbols so you can follow along when your friend shares their results.

- **Understand the testing process.** Hearing tests use both air and bone conduction to determine whether hearing loss is conductive, sensorineural, or mixed.

- **Recognize that hearing tests can be tiring and emotional.** They often bring a person face to face with their hearing challenges, which can stir feelings of frustration, anxiety, or sadness. Your patience and encouragement can make a big difference.

ALLY INSIGHTS

- How comfortable do I feel reading or discussing an audiogram?

- Does my loved one understand their audiogram enough to explain what their results mean in everyday terms?

- How might knowing the basics of air conduction vs. bone conduction help me understand their experience better?

In *Becoming Hearing Empowered*, your friend with hearing loss is completing an activity called **Plot Your Audiogram**. If they've had their hearing tested and obtained a copy of their audiogram, they use it to plot their hearing thresholds. If not, they practice on a sample audiogram included in the journal.

Because you don't have an audiogram, show support instead:

- Ask: "Would you like to share your audiogram with me?"

- Show genuine interest in how their results affect real-life listening situations, beyond what the graph shows.

- Affirm their effort in tracking and understanding their hearing health.

- Ask: "How do you feel when you have a hearing test?" to open the door for conversation.

Section 5: Hearing Testing (Part 3)

ALLY PERSPECTIVE: WHY THIS MATTERS

Knowing whether hearing loss is conductive, sensorineural, or mixed helps you understand why different treatments or technologies are recommended. Recognizing the role of pure tone average (PTA), speech reception threshold (SRT), and word recognition (WR) scores gives you a clearer picture of how much your friend with hearing loss understands speech, not just hear sounds, so you better support them in everyday conversations and medical decisions.

Types of Hearing Loss

Recall there are three types of hearing loss: conductive, sensorineural, and mixed. Based on the audiogram, audiologists determine the type of hearing loss by comparing air conduction and bone conduction test results. With this information, they identify whether the cause exists in the outer/ middle ear, the inner ear, or both.

Conductive hearing loss will show bone conduction test results as better than air conduction test results. This is referred to as an **air-bone gap**. It means that when tested with air conduction (using earphones or ear inserts that send sound through the outer, middle, and inner ear), the results indicate hearing loss. But when tested with bone conduction (using the headband bone conductor that sends sound directly to the cochlea), the results are much better. This shows the difficulty isn't in the cochlea. The problem occurs before sound reaches the inner ear.

Sensorineural hearing loss will show relatively the same test results for both air conduction and bone conduction. There is no air-bone gap. Both test types reveal hearing loss, confirming the issue is located in the cochlea.

Mixed hearing loss shows an air-bone gap for some frequencies, but not for others.

Pure Tone Average (PTA)

The pure tone average (PTA) is a calculation used to estimate how well a person hears the frequencies most commonly used in spoken language. It is a shorthand way of describing hearing loss that doesn't paint the full picture, but it is used frequently, so understanding what it means is valuable.

The PTA is calculated by taking the average hearing threshold levels across 4 frequencies: 500, 1000, 2000, and 4000 Hz. In other words, the decibel levels reported at these 4 frequencies are added together and then divided by 4.

For example: If an audiogram shows thresholds of 500 Hz = 20 dB, 1000 Hz = 35 dB, 2000 Hz = 50 dB, 4000 Hz = 70 dB, the PTA would be: 20 + 35 + 50 + 70 = 175 ÷ 4 = 44 dB

This number is used to describe the overall degree of hearing loss in that ear. In this case, 44 dB would fall into the moderate hearing loss range.

Speech Discrimination Tests

There are two main speech discrimination tests used in hearing evaluations: speech reception threshold (SRT) and word recognition score (WR).

Speech Reception Threshold (SRT): The SRT measures the quietest/softest volume at which a person hears and understands a 2-syllable word. The audiologist asks them to repeat words like baseball, hotdog, airplane, and bathtub. The softest level at which they repeat these words with 50% accuracy is their SRT. For example, an SRT of 50 dB means they were able to understand 50% of the words heard at 50 dB loudness.

Word Recognition Score (WR): The WR shows how well someone understands spoken words. Words are presented at levels that compensate for the frequencies missed in pure tone testing. Essentially, it tests comprehension when listening with optimal amplification. The audiologist says or plays a list of single-syllable words, and the person repeats them. The percentage of correct answers is the WR score. For example, if they correctly repeated 20 of 25 words, their WR = 80%.

ALLY IN ACTION

- **Ask your loved one:** "Do you know your word recognition score? What does it mean for everyday conversation?"

- **At the next audiology visit**, request that the audiologist explain SRT and WR results in practical terms, not just percentages. Ask: "What does this mean for understanding speech at a dinner table versus a quiet room?"

- **When they say "I heard you but didn't understand,"** believe them.

- Have I ever thought, or said, "But you heard me!" when they asked for clarification? What was I assuming in that moment?

- If their word recognition score is 65%, that means they miss roughly 1 in 3 words. How would I feel trying to follow a conversation with every third word missing?

In *Becoming Hearing Empowered*, your loved one completes an activity called **TYPE, PTA, SRT, AND WR**. They use their audiogram results to determine their type of hearing loss, calculate their pure tone average, and find their speech reception threshold and word recognition scores for each ear.

These numbers matter, but they don't define your loved one's worth or potential. If they choose to share their results, ask: "What do these numbers help you understand about your daily experience, and what do they leave out?"

This question acknowledges that test scores capture only part of the picture. If they don't know their SRT or WR scores, encourage them to request these tests at their next appointment. They provide valuable insight into real-world comprehension that pure tone testing alone cannot reveal.

Section 6: Describing Hearing Loss

ALLY PERSPECTIVE: WHY THIS MATTERS

Describing hearing loss accurately helps move past the myth that it's just about turning the volume up or down. Knowing terms that describe degree, type, and configuration of hearing loss gives you the language to understand your loved one's challenges more clearly and to support them in explaining their needs to others.

The experience of hearing loss is complicated. Many people imagine hearing loss to be a simple change in overall volume, like listening to the radio then turning the volume knob down a few notches. The music sounds the same, except every pitch and note is a little quieter than it was before.

If this were the case, hearing aids would act as a simple volume dial and, once everything was louder, hearing and understanding would be clear. Along the same lines, deafness is inaccurately imagined as pressing a "mute" button.

In actuality, hearing loss is complex. For example:

With **unilateral hearing loss** (one ear only), a person has difficulty locating sounds because one side doesn't provide the same input. Functionally, this makes group discussions harder, especially if they rely on lipreading but aren't able to quickly identify who is speaking.

With a **high frequency hearing loss**, a person misses the higher-pitched sounds of words (/k/, /t/, /s/, /f/, /th/, /sh/, /h/, /wh/), creating an auditory puzzle with missing pieces: "Wel_ome _o chapter _ree, earing Lo 101, __ere you _ill learn _e ba_i _ien_e of earing lo..."

A more accurate way of describing hearing loss uses the information provided in an audiogram. Generally, there are five main components to a comprehensive hearing loss description: **stability, laterality, type, degree, and configuration.**

Stability of Hearing Loss

Hearing loss isn't always permanent, and it doesn't always stay the same year after year. Terms used include:

- Permanent: not expected to change or improve.

- Progressive: worsening over time, and expected to continue.

- Fluctuating: alternating between better and worse.

- Stable: no significant change based on recent testing.

Laterality of Hearing Loss

- Unilateral: hearing loss in one ear.

- Bilateral: hearing loss in both ears.

Degrees of Hearing Loss

Hearing loss is described on a spectrum from **slight to profound**. Marks on the audiogram indicate the lowest volume (dB) at which a sound at a given frequency (Hz) is detected.

-10 to 15 dB = Normal, 16 to 25 dB = Slight, 26 to 40 dB = Mild, 41 to 55 dB = Moderate, 56 to 70 dB = Moderately severe, 71 to 90 dB = Severe, 91 dB and above = Profound

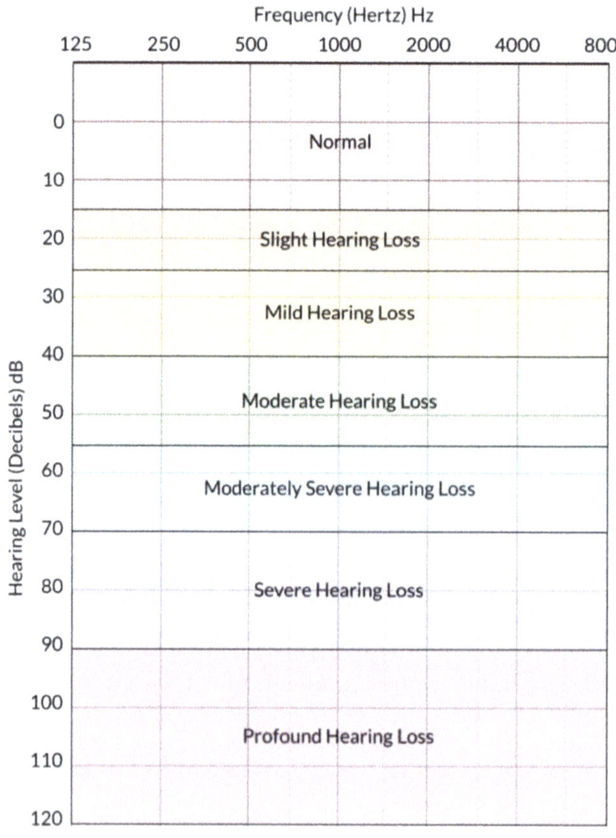

Configuration of Hearing Loss

When the symbols across frequencies on the audiogram are connected, the **shape of the line** shows the configuration:

- Flat: about the same across all frequencies.

- Sloping: better hearing at low frequencies, poorer at high frequencies.

- Rising: poorer at low frequencies, better at high.

- Cookie bite: poorer in the mid frequencies, better at low and high.

Hearing Loss Descriptions

Using the five elements—stability, laterality, type, degree, and configuration—creates a more precise description. Examples include:

- "Progressive unilateral sensorineural mild sloping to severe hearing loss in the right ear."

- "Permanent bilateral conductive moderate cookie bite hearing loss."

- "Fluctuating unilateral mixed severe rising to normal limits hearing loss in the left ear."

- "Permanent bilateral sensorineural flat moderate hearing loss."

"Percentage" of Hearing Loss

You've likely heard people say, "I'm 50% deaf in this ear, and 75% in my other." This is not an accurate way to describe hearing loss. It assumes hearing is just a volume dial. A better approach is to use audiogram terms, such as:

- "I have severe bilateral hearing loss in the mid and high frequencies. This means it is very difficult for me to hear all the sounds of speech even in the best of conditions, and much more difficult with background noise."

Simpler versions use PTA or WR scores:

- "I have a 50 dB hearing loss in my right ear and a 75 dB hearing loss in my left ear. I understand about 65% of speech in good conditions."

However, single numbers don't capture the whole picture. For example, difficulty with high frequencies or the extra challenge of background noise.

- **Skip the percentages.** Avoid describing hearing loss in percentages. It oversimplifies and can give the wrong impression.

- **Use accurate terms.** If your friend is comfortable sharing, practice using the correct terms from their audiogram, such as degree, type, and configuration.

- **Respect communication choices.** Your friend may describe their hearing loss differently depending on the audience: detailed with a doctor, simplified with a coworker, or minimal with a stranger.

- **Acknowledge the effort.** Even with hearing aids, missing certain sounds can make communication tiring. Patience and awareness go a long way.

- How does knowing about "degree," "configuration," and "laterality" change how I interpret my loved one's communication challenges?

- Is their hearing loss permanent, progressive, fluctuating? How does this change how I view their hearing loss?

- How do I adapt my own communication when I realize they are missing specific speech sounds?

In *Becoming Hearing Empowered*, your communication partner is completing a set of activities to describe their hearing loss in detail using their audiogram called **Describe Your Hearing Loss**. They may write comprehensive descriptions, PTA-based statements, or word recognition summaries.

To support them:

- Ask: "Would you like to share your hearing loss descriptions with me?"

- Listen without judgment, and respect whether they prefer technical or simple terms in different settings.

- Affirm the effort it takes to learn and use these terms.

- Practice ways you explain their hearing loss to others (with their permission), so you're ready to advocate when needed.

4 | the emotional impact of hearing loss

We were in the break room before the morning shift when it happened. Someone told a joke, everyone laughed, and Marcus leaned in: "What did he say?"

One of the guys waved a hand. "Never mind! It wasn't that funny."

The group moved on. Marcus smiled and nodded. But I saw his jaw tighten. I saw him stop trying to follow the conversation after that.

Later, in my office, I asked if he was okay. He shrugged. "I'm used to it."

But the way he said it—flat, resigned—told me he shouldn't have to be. And I wondered how many times I'd been the one to say "never mind" without thinking.

Section 1: First Steps

ALLY PERSPECTIVE: WHY THIS MATTERS

The emotional side of hearing loss is often overlooked, especially by those who haven't experienced it themselves. Unlike vision changes, which most people relate to easily and manage with glasses, hearing loss carries layers of emotion that people rarely discuss. Frustration, grief, and shame are often part of the experience for both the person with hearing loss and those who love them. Recognizing these feelings allows you to respond with compassion instead of quick fixes, and to remember that your steady, caring presence matters more than having all the answers.

This section is one of the hardest in the book. The emotional impact of hearing loss runs deep, and for many people, talking about it is painful. Your loved one likely carries unspoken frustration, grief, embarrassment, anger, fear, anxiety, regret, or shame that has built up over years of difficult experiences.

These emotions don't appear in isolation. They come from real life moments: being excluded from conversations, missing important details at work, feeling like a burden for asking someone to repeat, or being misunderstood when requesting accommodations. Over time, repeated experiences like these affect confidence, self-esteem, and even identity.

If you don't experience life with hearing loss, you likely find it difficult to understand how many emotions attach to this condition. The depth of emotion connected to hearing loss is often overlooked by those who haven't experienced it. After all, vision changes are so common. Practically everyone wears glasses or will need them eventually, and they're easily managed (most of the time) with corrective lenses. Because this type of vision loss is so familiar and fixable, people rarely talk about it as something that carries deep emotion. Hearing loss, however, is different. People hide its emotional weight, rarely acknowledge it, and even less often discuss it openly. No matter what the audiogram says about the degree of hearing loss, it can never be fully corrected by hearing aids or cochlear implants, and it significantly impacts access to communication and social connection. It creates acute frustration during the most pleasant social gatherings. It builds a solid wall of isolation just when human connection is most needed. Hearing loss wells up a red wave of anger in the midst of watching a movie because the caption timing is off. Many people experience fear because of their hearing loss: unable to hear someone walking behind them, unable to hear their child calling, unable to locate the source of an emergency siren. Hearing loss also leads to deep feelings of sadness or depression. Constant listening effort leaves a person exhausted, worried about standing out, or afraid of missing what others say. It's easy to feel lost in a sea of conversation and to start believing that quiet withdrawal is the only option.

Even so, the emotional weight doesn't stop with the person who has hearing loss. It also affects you. Many allies feel helpless watching their loved one struggle, frustrated when communication breaks down, or resentful when the effort feels one-sided. These reactions are normal. What matters is how you respond to them. Part of being an empowered ally is naming your own feelings and finding constructive ways to manage them, so you can keep showing up with compassion.

Two helpful tools are introduced in this book: **growth mindset** and **Cognitive Behavioral Theory (CBT)**. A growth mindset means believing that situations can change with new strategies, patience, and practice. Instead of "this will always be hopeless," a growth mindset says, "this is hard, but we can adapt and find new ways." CBT offers a way to understand how thoughts influence feelings, and feelings influence behaviors. Shifting the way you think about a situation creates space for more helpful emotions and healthier responses.

Recognizing and naming these emotions is not weakness; it's essential. Once acknowledged, they can be reframed using growth mindset and CBT, creating opportunities for healing and resilience.

This chapter's goal is to help you understand how deep the emotional impact of hearing loss goes, and to give you strategies to respond with compassion and strength. Some parts will feel heavy, but staying present with your loved one in their pain, without rushing to fix it, is one of the most powerful forms of support you offer.

- **Name emotions without blame.** Notice frustration, sadness, or anger (yours or theirs) and acknowledge them calmly.

- **Model growth mindset.** Say things like, "This is hard, but we'll keep trying new ways."

- **Create safe space.** Encourage breaks during emotional conversations and return when both of you feel ready.

- When my communication partner feels emotional about hearing loss, what feelings arise in me? Helplessness, frustration, urgency to fix?

- How do those feelings shape my response? Do I withdraw, criticize, or overcompensate?

- What supports or self-care practices help me stay compassionate when the emotional weight feels heavy?

In *Becoming Hearing Empowered*, your friend's journal activity, **Processing Negative Experiences**, where they are asked to revisit negative, and sometimes painful, hearing-loss-related experiences and document the details: who was there, what happened, what they thought, how they felt, and how they responded. This is often a very emotional exercise. What they write in this journal activity will be used to reframe the experience in a more positive and empowering way in Section 4.

To support them:

- Offer presence rather than solutions. Sometimes a listening ear is enough.

- Validate their courage: "Thank you for telling me. That sounds really painful."

- Respect their privacy if they choose not to share.

- Reinforce that this exercise is meant to give these negative experiences a space to exist outside of their mind and their heart, and they will be reframed into something positive and empowering in the upcoming sections.

Section 2: Cognitive Behavioral Theory

Understanding CBT gives you a window into why your loved one reacts strongly in certain moments. It's not just the behavior you see, but the thoughts and feelings behind it. Knowing this helps you respond with patience, reframe situations together, and support healthier patterns instead of frustration or withdrawal.

Cognitive Behavioral Theory (CBT) suggests that when anyone has an experience, their **thoughts lead to feelings, and those feelings lead to behaviors**. This is as true for your friend with hearing loss as it is for you.

The way a person interprets a situation influences how they feel about it, and how they feel shapes the way they act. Considering your friend's past experiences—their thoughts about them, how those thoughts made them feel, and how they responded—is an important step in recognizing why certain patterns repeat and how they change in the future. If the way they think about a situation shifts, it profoundly changes their emotional response and their choices about how to behave.

A Common Situation

Imagine your communication partner misses a joke and someone says, "never mind."

- **Thoughts:** "They can't be bothered to repeat it. I'm not important. They must think I'm stupid. They just don't get it."

- **Feelings:** Rejection, loneliness, anxiety, embarrassment, being discounted.

- **Behaviors:** Stop asking for repeats, smile and nod, avoid hanging out, withhold contributions.

A Growth Mindset Perspective

Now consider the same moment through the lens of a growth mindset, which assumes both you and others have the capacity to learn and change. One of the most powerful words to remember here is "yet." It reminds us that learning and change are still possible. That growth is just over the horizon.

Same scenario: someone says "never mind" when a joke is missed.

- **Thoughts:** "They probably don't know I have hearing loss. They likely don't realize how hurtful 'never mind' feels. They don't understand—yet."

- **Feelings:** Still some sting of being left out, but also a sense that this misunderstanding is "more about them than about me." If it's a new acquaintance, even hope that they could learn. Empowerment: instead of withdrawing, there's now room for growth.

- **Behaviors:** Speaking up, either in the moment ("Actually, could you please not say 'never mind' to me?"), or later ("My hearing loss causes me to miss things, and when you say, 'never mind' it takes away my ability to decide what is important and what isn't important to understand"). Or, "You probably don't realize this, but when people used to say that to me, I would withdraw and avoid being social. I enjoy being around you and I want you to understand what I need so we can communicate better."

In this reframed version, your loved one takes a proactive role in advocating for themselves. They don't control how the other person will respond, but instead of retreating into silence, they've created an opportunity for connection, and for that person to become an ally too.

Fixed vs. Growth Mindset Thoughts

Negative or irrational thoughts often surface more easily when someone is tired, hungry, or has faced the same situation repeatedly. Common fixed-mindset thoughts include:

- "This always happens to me. It must be my fault."

- "Hearing people will never understand."

- "Why do I even try?"

- But positive or open-minded thoughts shift the experience:

- "This happens often. If I try a new strategy, will it get better?"

- "Many hearing people haven't had the chance to know someone who is deaf, so of course it's hard for them to relate."

- "I am an agent of change."

Knowing how powerful these shifts are helps you respond more compassionately when your loved one gets caught in the cycle of negative thoughts and feelings.

- **Don't dismiss reactions.** If your communication partner seems hurt by something like "never mind," recognize there's a deeper chain of thoughts → feelings → behaviors happening beneath the surface.

- **Model reframing.** Use language like: "They probably don't understand yet" or "Let's try another approach next time."

- **Practice patience.** Remember that fatigue, stress, or repeated experiences make negative thoughts louder.

- When my loved one reacts strongly, do I focus only on the behavior (withdrawing, snapping) instead of the feelings and thoughts behind it?

- How do I usually interpret situations where someone says something dismissive like "never mind"?

- Do I fall into fixed mindset thoughts myself ("This will always be stressful")? How do I shift to growth mindset thinking?

In *Becoming Hearing Empowered*, your friend with hearing loss completes an activity called **Cognitive Behavioral Theory Illustrated**. They map out how negative thoughts lead to feelings and behaviors, and then reimagine how positive thoughts reshape the cycle. An example of this journal activity is found at the end of this section.

To support them:

- Ask: "Would you like to share your drawing or reflections with me?"

- Notice how their negative-thought cycle compares with yours in similar situations.

- Affirm the effort it takes to face those thoughts on paper.

- Offer to share your own quick example of a thought → feeling → behavior chain, showing that this process is universal.

Thoughts (positive reframes)
- If they know I have a hearing loss, they will want to help.
- People are used to a fast pace — they will appreciate slowing down!
- People have a lot on their mind — It's easy to forget I have a hearing loss.
- People will appreciate being reminded — these people that love me.
- People want to help — they don't know how yet.

Feelings
- Hopeful
- Confident
- Encouraged
- Understanding
- Patient
- Supported
- EMPOWERED
- Proud
- Unashamed
- LOVED
- Reinforced
- Mindful

Behaviors
- Quick to remind people
- Live in the moment → mindful communication
- Speak up — once, twice OPTE
- Advocate more often
- Support others
- Have more energy for other activities.
- Engage
- Provide positive feedback and appreciation!!

Thoughts ➡ Feelings ➡ Behaviors

Thoughts
- Most people don't care.
- No one wants to help me.
- Everyone is grumpy & impatient.
- People don't think enough about what I need. (I'm always thinking about what THEY need.)
- If they know I have a hearing loss, they will think I'm dumb/incapable/a burden.

Feelings
- SAD
- Left out.
- Lonely
- Angry!
- Forgotten
- Less than.
- HURT
- Neglected/Ignored.
- Looked down on
- LOST
- Disrespected.

Behaviors
- Withdraw.
- Distract myself from the activity/conversation feelings
- Wait for someone to notice.
- Stop caring about what the other person needs.
- Don't give eye contact.
- Leave.
- Yell, cry, storm out.
- Just sit here.
- Pretend/Bluff.
- Snap back.

Section 3: CBT Practice

Practicing CBT helps both you and your loved one see how a small shift in thoughts changes feelings and actions. By reframing together, you turn frustrating or discouraging moments into opportunities for patience, understanding, and connection.

Cognitive Behavioral Theory (CBT) becomes most powerful when it's practiced. Today's focus is applying it to real-life situations.

Scenario 1: From Your Loved One's Perspective

Imagine your friend with hearing loss is in a grocery store. They ask the clerk to repeat something, and instead the clerk shouts loudly: "HOW ARE YOU? DID YOU FIND EVERYTHING YOU NEEDED?" The sudden loudness and exaggerated tone don't help them understand; instead, it draws unwanted attention and feels embarrassing or demeaning.

- **Possible thoughts:** "That was so rude. Everyone's staring. They think I'm dumb. This always happens."

- **Possible feelings:** Embarrassment, anger, humiliation, defeat.

- **Possible behaviors:** Avoid eye contact, hurry out, choose self-checkout in the future, internalize shame.

Now imagine reframing the thoughts:

- "Maybe the clerk has a relative with hearing loss, and this is what works for them."

- "Maybe the clerk is having a rough day, and their tone wasn't about me."

- "Even if they were being unkind, that doesn't define me."

With these new thoughts, the feelings shift: less humiliation, more curiosity, or even empowerment. And behaviors shift too: staying calm, explaining their needs, or deciding to advocate in that moment.

This helps you see how a single thought pattern determines whether your friend withdraws in shame or speaks up with confidence.

Scenario 2: From Your Perspective

Now let's apply CBT to your own experience. Imagine you've repeated yourself three times at dinner and your communication partner still doesn't catch what you said.

- Initial thoughts: "This is exhausting. They're not even trying."

- Feelings: Frustration, resentment, discouragement.

- Behaviors: Shutting down, avoiding conversation, or speaking less often.

Now reframe:

- "We're both tired; it makes sense this is harder right now."

- "They're still engaged. That's why they keep asking me to repeat."

- "We're learning strategies that will make this easier."

New thoughts lead to new feelings: more patience, compassion, hope. These lead to new behaviors: calmly repeating again, offering to write it down, or suggesting a quick pause so both of you can reset.

- **Practice reframing together.** After tough interactions, gently ask: "What thought went through your head? How could we reframe it?"

- **Catch your own thoughts.** Notice when frustration rises and ask yourself: "What else could be true here?"

- **Assume positive intent.** Even if someone seems rude, experiment with giving them the benefit of the doubt to see how it changes your feelings.

- Do I tend to assume the worst about people's intentions (i.e., "they don't care"), or am I willing to experiment with more generous interpretations?

- How do my automatic thoughts at the dinner table, family gatherings, or social events affect my willingness to keep engaging?

- What feelings do I want to bring into these situations, and what thoughts would support those feelings?

In *Becoming Hearing Empowered*, your loved one completes an activity called **Cognitive Behavioral Theory Practice**. They apply CBT to scenarios like the grocery store, exploring how negative thoughts shape feelings and behaviors; and how positive reframing changes the outcome.

To support them:

- Ask: "Would you like to share your reflections?"

- Listen without judgment if they describe painful feelings.

- Affirm their courage: "I can see how hard this was to write about. Thank you for sharing."

- Try your own quick CBT reflection on a situation you've faced. Show that reframing is a shared skill.

Section 4: Reclaiming and Reframing

ALLY PERSPECTIVE: WHY THIS MATTERS

This exercise is about taking a painful moment, recognizing it, and then reshaping it with new thoughts that create strength and hope. Practicing this yourself shows your loved one that growth and resilience are possible on both sides of the relationship.

"Reclaiming and Reframing" is a process of taking a painful experience, honoring it, and then deliberately reshaping it with new thoughts that allow for strength, courage, and hope. For your friend with hearing loss, this activity is deeply personal, as it asks them to revisit difficult memories and shift how they hold them.

But this process is not just for the person with hearing loss. You may also carry heavy feelings: embarrassment when communication fails in public, frustration when you repeat yourself, or even resentment when effort feels one-sided. Reclaiming and Reframing invites you too to plant those negative experiences in the "soil" of your awareness, and then grow something new from them.

The steps are:

- **Identify the experience.** Recall a moment that felt discouraging, embarrassing, or frustrating.

- **Name the thoughts.** Write down the negative self-talk or assumptions that grew out of that moment.

- **Acknowledge the feelings.** Recognize how those thoughts shaped emotions like shame, anger, or defeat.

- **Reframe with new thoughts.** Above those negative thoughts, write alternative perspectives; ones rooted in compassion, patience, or growth mindset.

- **Visualize new growth.** Imagine the new behaviors and feelings that grow out of these reframed thoughts: strength, courage, hope. Draw or write symbols of resilience: a tree, a flower, a rainbow, bold words of affirmation.

The purpose is not to erase what happened, but to reclaim agency. Even from painful experiences, choose to grow something new.

- **Reflect on your own moments.** Think about times you've felt embarrassed, impatient, or misunderstood in your role as an ally.

- **Shift your mindset.** Use these experiences to move from resentment ("This always happens") to empowerment ("I will respond differently next time").

- **Model shared growth.** Share a small example with your communication partner to show that self-awareness and change are something you're both practicing.

ALLY INSIGHTS

- What's one situation related to hearing loss that I still carry as frustration or embarrassment?

- What negative thoughts grew from that experience?

- How do I reframe those thoughts into more compassionate or constructive ones?

- What behaviors change if I carry those new thoughts forward?

In *Becoming Hearing Empowered*, your friend with hearing loss completes the activity **Reclaiming and Reframing**, transforming painful experiences into symbols of resilience and growth. This is often an emotional process. An example of this journal activity is found at the end of this section.

To support them:

- Ask: "Would you like to share your reframed thoughts or artwork?"

- Listen without judgment, affirming their courage to face hard memories.

- Say something supportive, like: "I see how much strength this took. Thank you for trusting me."

- Respect their privacy if they keep it personal. The act of doing the exercise is powerful enough.

If you've done your own **Reclaiming and Reframing** exercise, share that too. Showing vulnerability helps normalize the process and strengthens the sense that both of you are growing together.

PRIDE
Self-Respect
VOICE
BRAVE
Empowered
Important
Reclaiming and Reframing
What he did had nothing to do with me.
The class knew he was a jerk.
He needed me to push back so that he knew he was wrong.
Other students will benefit from me being a role model.
My understanding MATTERS!
I deserved to learn like everyone else in the class!
EXPERIENCE: My college professor mocked me in class.
THOUGHTS: He is so mean. He wants to humiliate me in front of everyone. I'm an idiot for speaking up. Everyone thinks I'm annoying and self-centered. I asked for too much
FEELINGS: Embarrassed! Ashamed. My understanding is not important. Insignificant. Alone. Humiliated. Angry! UNSAFE! At a disadvantage.
BEHAVIORS: Stop asking for what I need. Stop talking and stop participating. Sit toward the back. Avoid seeing or talking to him. Avoid future professors!

Section 5: Internalized Stigma & Positive Experiences

When your loved one hesitates to speak up or feels embarrassed about their devices, it is likely the weight of stigma, not a lack of effort. Recognizing this helps you respond with compassion, while also affirming their resilience and celebrating the strengths that have grown through their experience

Internalized Stigma

Internalized stigma happens when someone with hearing loss absorbs negative stereotypes or cultural messages and comes to believe them as true. Society often suggests that hearing loss is something to be hidden: "Only old people wear hearing aids," "people with hearing disabilities are not as smart as hearing people," or "devices should be invisible so no one notices." Over time, these messages undermine confidence, increase shame, and make it harder for your friend to ask for what they need.

When your communication partner hesitates to disclose their hearing loss, avoids advocating for accommodations, or feels embarrassment about assistive devices, it is not a personal failing. It is the weight of internalized stigma.

Positive Experiences

Hearing loss is not defined only by stigma or struggle. It also brings unexpected gifts: resilience built through challenge, empathy arising from past struggles with hearing, friendships formed in supportive communities, and even career paths inspired by lived experience.

Celebrating these positives doesn't mean ignoring the hard parts. It means balancing the narrative. Naming resilience, courage, and community alongside the pain allows for a fuller, more accurate picture of what life with hearing loss holds.

- **Challenge stigma when you see it.** Speak up when others make dismissive or ageist remarks.

- **Affirm positive identity.** Tell your loved one how you see their resilience, creativity, or empathy.

- **Celebrate wins.** Recognize moments when hearing loss led to a new friend, an advocacy success, or a courageous action.

- **Model acceptance.** Treat hearing devices and accommodations as normal and valuable, not as something to hide.

- Have I unintentionally echoed stigma, like suggesting my friend's hearing devices are "barely noticeable" instead of affirming them proudly?

- What negative cultural messages about hearing loss have I absorbed without realizing it?

- What positive qualities do I see in my loved one that grew because of their hearing loss?

In *Becoming Hearing Empowered*, your friend with hearing loss works on two journal activities:

Internalized Stigma

- They write a negative stereotype (i.e., "asking for accommodations is embarrassing") in the center.

- Around it, they surround the message with affirmations and positive images that contradict it.

- An example of this journal activity is found on the following page.

Positive Experiences

- They describe or express times when hearing loss led to something good: meeting new people, demonstrating courage, or influencing others in a positive way.

- They use words, drawings, or color to celebrate those experiences.

To support them:

- Ask: "Would you like to share one of your stigma circles or positive experiences?"

- Listen without judgment, affirming their courage in facing painful messages and their pride in celebrating strengths.

- Make your own stigma circle. Choose a negative message you've encountered in your own life (it doesn't have to be about hearing loss) and surround it with affirmations. Doing this side by side shows solidarity and helps normalize the practice.

- Create your own "positive experiences" list about what you have gained through walking alongside them: new communities, empathy, or resilience. Sharing your perspective reinforces that hearing loss has shaped both of your lives in meaningful ways.

- Echo their affirmations in daily life so positive counter-messages become reinforced outside the journal pages.

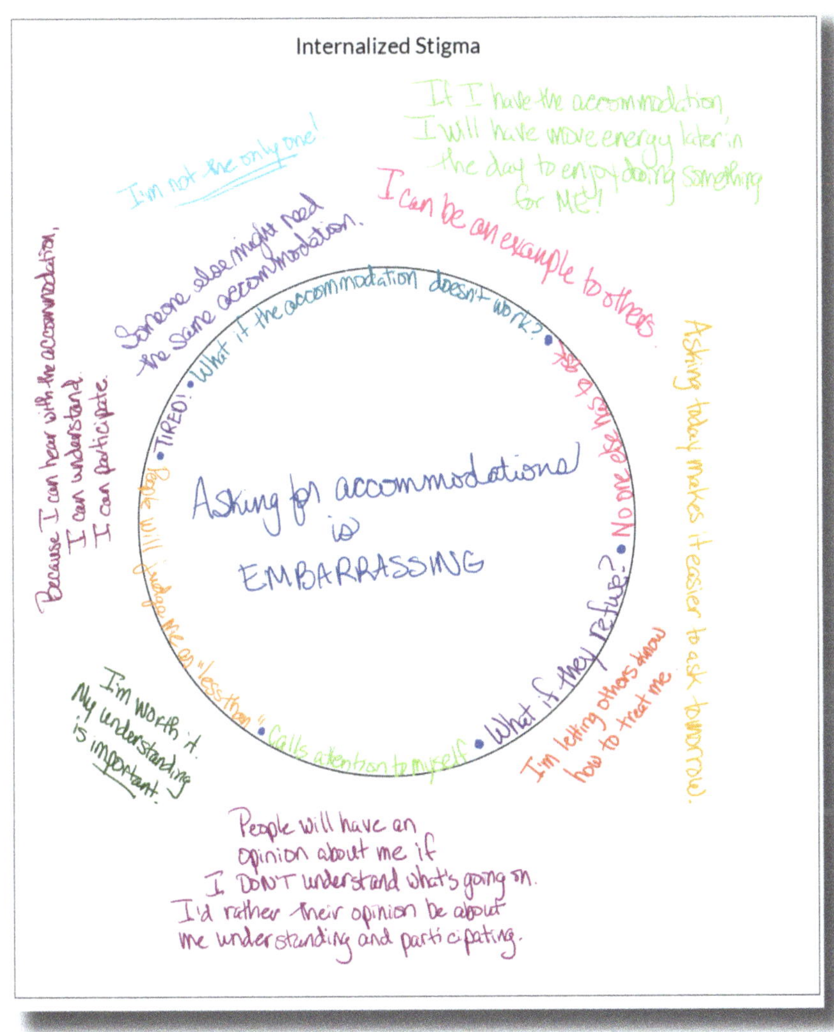

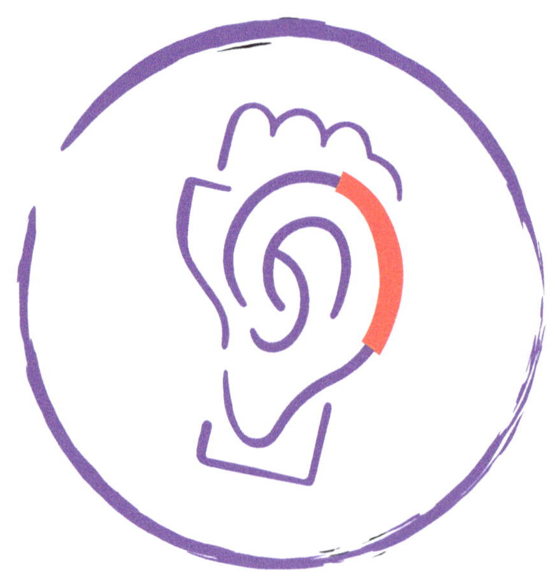

5 | identity & self-love

I walked into her room and found my 15-year-old daughter standing at the mirror, brushing her hair forward over her ears.

"What are you doing?" I asked.

She didn't look at me. "Just... making sure they don't show."

Her hearing aids. She was hiding her hearing aids before the homecoming dance.

I wanted to say, "No one will care" or "You look beautiful." But I could see on her face that she cared. That this wasn't about vanity. It was about not wanting to be seen as different. Not wanting to explain. Not wanting the first thing her classmates noticed to be the devices in her ears.

She'd only been wearing them for a few months. She was still figuring out who she was with them.

I didn't say anything. I just told her she looked perfect. But I carried that moment with me for a long time.

Section 1: The Acceptance Continuum

ALLY PERSPECTIVE: WHY THIS MATTERS

Hearing loss doesn't just affect communication. It affects how a person sees themself. Identity is the collection of traits, roles, and experiences that shape how someone understands who they are. For people with hearing loss, self-identity often includes the struggle between hiding it and learning to embrace it as part of their wholeness.

Whether your loved one has had hearing loss since childhood or developed it later in life, they likely struggle with fully accepting it. It is actually quite common for someone with hearing loss to deny it to others, and even to themselves. Negative experiences and internalized stigma create shame and embarrassment about something completely outside of their control. The work you read about in earlier chapters is the foundation for understanding how stigma affects daily life. As your loved one continues to process those emotions, it is also important to recognize how hearing loss impacts their identity and how they feel about themselves.

Hearing loss is a unique kind of disability because it directly affects communication with others. The hearing world we live in is fast-paced and impatient. There is an unspoken expectation among hearing people that daily interactions at work, in the grocery store, and at home will be quick, invisible, and efficient. Spoken languages are filled with slang, dialect, idioms, and imperfectly produced words spoken through the mumbly, often-obscured mouths of humans multitasking as they walk, eat, drink, or brush their teeth. Any degree of hearing loss significantly affects the ability to understand speech in noise, and our world is defined by noise.

This means your communication partner's ability to understand what someone is saying is only partially in their control. They have state-of-the-art hearing technology and are highly skilled at lipreading, but if the person they're communicating with doesn't make adjustments, breakdowns will occur. Herein lies the bridge that only they can extend: "I have a hearing loss…" "I am deaf…" "I can't hear you…" Whether they offer that information or not, their hearing loss is still a part of how they are perceived. The person they are communicating with sees a signal: either they know your friend has hearing loss because it was disclosed, or they sense "something" is making communication more difficult.

This isn't always malicious; it's often just the brain making a quick calculation when the natural flow of conversation breaks down. But these moments are painful. Your friend with hearing loss feels offended if people assume they aren't smart, or ignored if the conversation simply moves on without them. Of course, some people do behave in offensive or dismissive ways, but most of the time, communication involving hearing loss veers off course unintentionally.

This is where your role as an ally matters. Your loved one can take responsibility for explaining their needs, but they can't keep every conversation on track alone. Communication is a shared responsibility. They can disclose their hearing loss, ask for clearer speech, or request repetition, but the person they communicate with also must adjust. Think of it like learning to drive a manual car when you've only driven automatic. It feels awkward at first, but it's a skill you can learn. People's willingness to change how they communicate is just as important as your communication partner's willingness to disclose.

Self-disclosure of hearing loss is not a "one and done" task. It can happen multiple times a day, in new settings and with new people. Because hearing loss is often invisible, others don't realize adjustments are needed until your loved one speaks up. This was especially clear during the COVID-19 pandemic, when masks removed access to lipreading.

For your loved one, hearing loss is not just a medical condition, it's part of their identity. Self-disclosure improves communication. Self-advocacy builds confidence. And when you respond with patience and adjustments, you reinforce that they belong and that communication is worth the effort. In this chapter, you'll learn how identity and personality intersect with hearing loss, and how to support both self-acceptance and empowerment.

Denial vs Acceptance

For many people with hearing loss, self-acceptance doesn't happen overnight. It's a gradual process, often marked by setbacks, progress, and new realizations. At times, someone may try to hide or ignore their hearing loss. At other times, they may speak openly about it and feel empowered to advocate.

Maybe your friend has accepted their hearing loss and is ready to move forward. Or they might still be in a place where it feels easier to think of themselves as "not really" having a hearing loss, or that it doesn't really impact their life. Wherever they fall on the continuum of denial to acceptance, the truth is, most people with hearing loss shift back and forth depending on the situation.

Acceptance often varies with context. Your friend might feel comfortable being open at home but hesitates to disclose at school or work. They may freely share their hearing loss with close friends, but prefer to keep it private with casual acquaintances. It probably depends on who they are talking to, and what kind of listening environment they're in.

Regardless of where they land on any given day, that's OK. What matters is recognizing that their feelings about hearing loss directly affect both their happiness and their ability to connect with others, including you.

Here's the challenge: learning about communication strategies and accommodations is only helpful if the person with hearing loss feels ready to use them. If denial is holding them back, they may resist asking for captions, requesting repetition of information, or disclosing their hearing loss, even when it would make life easier.

Understanding this dynamic helps you respond with empathy rather than frustration. Instead of assuming they "don't want help," recognize that acceptance is a process, not a single moment. If your friend is reluctant to acknowledge their hearing loss, it doesn't mean they're "in denial" or stubborn. It means they're in a stage where self-protection feels safer than visibility.

ALLY IN ACTION

- **Notice, don't push:** Acceptance shifts with safety and support. Meet them where they are.

- **Affirm progress:** Celebrate small steps toward openness.

- **Avoid minimizing:** Never dismiss their experience as "no big deal."

- **Be consistent:** Steady acceptance builds trust and confidence.

- Where do I think my loved one is on the acceptance continuum right now?

- How do I respond when they downplay or hide their hearing loss?

- What do I do to create a safe environment that encourages self-acceptance?

In *Becoming Hearing Empowered*, your friend with hearing loss reflects on where they land along **The Acceptance Continuum**.

Ask:

- "Would you like to share where you see yourself on the continuum?"

- "What situations make it harder to accept, or be open about, your hearing loss?"

- "What helps you feel more comfortable being open about it?"

Section 2: Words & Labels

Words carry power. The terms your loved one chooses are not just labels. They are part of how they define themselves. Honoring their language choices shows respect for their dignity and reinforces that their identity belongs to them, not to medical systems or outside opinions.

Understanding Common Phrases and Labels

We're going to discuss common words and labels people use to describe hearing loss, looking at both their literal meaning and how those words have been understood within the d/Deaf and Hard of Hearing communities. Before we examine specific terms, it's helpful to understand that not all labels describe the same thing.

Medical Labels vs. Identity Labels

Medical labels and identity labels don't always align, and understanding this distinction is important for allies.

A person might be considered *deaf* based on an audiogram, reflecting the medical degree of hearing loss, but personally identifies as *Hard of Hearing* because they communicate primarily through spoken language, use hearing technology, and rely on visual cues.

Conversely, someone medically described as having a moderate hearing loss (often considered "hard of hearing) identifies as Deaf because they use a signed language and participate primarily within the Deaf community.

Medical labels describe auditory thresholds, while identity labels reflect lived experience, communication choices, and cultural alignment. Both serve different purposes: one clinical, the other personal and social.

Understanding this difference helps set the stage for the terms you'll encounter next, and why some words carry positive, negative, or shifting meanings depending on context and identity.

Hearing Impaired, Hearing Impairment

The terms "hearing impaired" and "hearing impairment" are frequently used in the medical, legal, and educational fields, and they usually are used as an umbrella term under which all degrees of hearing loss fit. Literally, it means "not able to hear well." Merriam-Webster defines "impaired" as "being in an imperfect or weakened state or condition: such as diminished in function or ability," and this statement is actually true for the physical condition of the hearing anatomy; however, many d/Deaf and Hard of Hearing people consider the term "hearing impaired" offensive because the words "imperfect" and "weakened" applied to the person are inaccurate.

Hard of Hearing

"Hard of hearing" is a widely preferred way to identify someone with hearing loss. Generally, "hard of hearing" refers to having a "defective but functional" sense of hearing. This usually means mild to moderate or moderately severe hearing loss that makes understanding speech difficult, but still possible with any number of supports, including technology and/or accommodations.

Hearing Loss

I've been using this term widely as an umbrella label that encompasses all levels of hearing loss, from slight to profound; however, it does have some negative connotations that are important to mention. The word "loss" generally refers to having lost something, and for those who acquired hearing loss later in life, it may feel like a good fit. But for those born with diminished or inability to hear, nothing was lost because you can't lose something you never had. "Loss" can also be a word that indicates deficiency. So for those reasons, "hearing loss" is not always preferred. Still, there are not yet other universally accepted options to replace it.

Hearing Disabled, Hearing Disability

Similar to the rejection of "impairment," there have been negative feelings about using the word "disability" to describe hearing loss. "Disability" indicates the inability to do major activities of daily living. Especially for those in the Deaf community that use signed language, there really is nothing a Deaf person can't do, except hear. With sign language and new technology, they argue there isn't a necessity to be able to actually hear.

However, many people in the wider disabled community are speaking out about living life with disabilities, and are reclaiming the use of "disabled" and "disability" as appropriate, and even preferred. They have challenged ableism by refusing to hide or be shamed by stigma that used to be associated with those terms. One reason is because the word disability connects people to a larger group, many of whom are advocating for accessibility in one way or another. "Disability" and "individuals with disabilities" are also the terms used in the (US) laws written to protect rights and provide equal access.

deaf (also known as "little d" deaf)

The term "deaf" is frequently used and is considered a preferred label in the d/Deaf and Hard of Hearing community. The medical, legal and educational communities tend to define "deaf" or "deafness" as a hearing impairment so severe, with or without amplification, that speech understanding is very poor. So, in general, people with severe to profound hearing loss in most frequencies. The general population also widely views "deaf" to mean literal inability to hear.

However, in recent years, "deaf" is being used as an all-inclusive term for all levels of hearing loss, including deaf, hard of hearing and deafblind. It is not yet widely recognized in general society, so people may be confused when what they understand to be a "hard of hearing" person uses "deaf" as an identifying label.

Oral-deaf

The term *oral-deaf* is often used to describe someone with severe to profound hearing loss who primarily uses spoken language rather than sign language to communicate. While *deaf* by itself often refers simply to the degree of hearing loss, *oral-deaf* adds clarity about communication preference and access. People who identify as oral-deaf may rely on hearing technology such as hearing aids or cochlear implants, along with speechreading and other strategies. This label helps distinguish their experience from that of individuals who identify as culturally Deaf and communicate mainly through sign language within the Deaf community.

Deaf (also known as "big d" Deaf)

"Deaf" with a capital D is widely recognized to describe the community of people who use signed languages and participate as members of the Deaf community. American Sign Language, British Sign Language and many others are complex and full languages, and those that use them have a rich and deep culture, created by close relationships within the community, complete with history and traditions. It is possible for a person with mild to moderate hearing loss to identify as Deaf if they actively participate in the Deaf community, and for a person with severe to profound hearing loss who doesn't use sign language and primarily functions in the hearing world to identify as hard of hearing or oral-deaf.

Acquired Deafness, Late-Deafened, Sudden Deafness, Sudden Hearing Loss (SHL), Sudden Sensorineural Hearing Loss (SSHL)

These terms are frequently used to describe loss of hearing that occurred or developed some time during the lifespan, but it was not present at birth. This is a significant distinction, because someone who was living in the hearing world, using spoken language, loses their ability to hear and is faced with serious, devastating communication challenges. When a hearing loss occurs rapidly, it is considered sudden hearing loss or sudden deafness.

Congenital Deafness

Hearing loss that is present from birth and is not necessarily hereditary. A child born hard of hearing or deaf is often provided with early interventions and supported with extra services in K-12 school. For some children, they learn sign language at an early age at home and/or school.

Outdated Terms: Hearing Handicap, Hearing Disorder, Hearing Deficit, Hearing Defect, Hearing Abnormality, Deaf and Dumb, Deaf-Mute

These terms are generally considered outdated and are often seen as offensive. It is important to recognize the history of labels for the deaf, many of which have been harmful or inaccurate. "Dumb" is a multiple meaning word that means "lacking intelligence," however, it also means "mute" or "lacking the ability to speak." During the early 19th century, "deaf and dumb" was a widely used descriptor for a person unable to speak, but by the end of the 20th century, the offensiveness of dumb was widely recognized. The people of the Deaf community continue to fight for recognition as highly capable and intelligent with a complex language and culture, and we need to be aware of the power of words and labels.

Person-First Language and Identity-First Language

There is debate in the disabled community about person-first and identity-first language. **Person-first language** describes the person, then the disability:

- A person with a hearing disability.

- A person who is deaf.

- I have a hearing disability.

Identity-first language describes the disability as part of the person:

- A hearing disabled person.

- A deaf person.

- I am hearing disabled.

Person-first language was once considered the politically correct preference. Its intention was to demonstrate that a person is a person before their disability or diagnosis. However, disabled people began to reject this way of referring to themselves. Having a disability is different from having a medical illness, and person-first language treats having a disability like having an ailment or disease.

- I have COVID-19.

- I have cancer.

- I have a hearing impairment.

While disabilities are diagnosed, they are not the same as an illness because the disability isn't something to be cured, nor is it contagious. A person's disability is an integral part of who they are, and it becomes part of their identity; therefore, identity-first language is frequently preferred.

- I am disabled.

- I am autistic.

- I am deaf.

Decisions, Decisions

Choosing words and labels is not just a matter of vocabulary. It is about identity, dignity, and self-definition. For your friend with hearing loss, deciding whether to call themselves Deaf, deaf, hard of hearing, late-deafened, or something else may carry some emotional weight.

Your role is not to decide for them or suggest which label "sounds better." Your role is to listen, respect, and use the language they choose. Even if you've heard other terms used by professionals, family members, or in the media, it's important to honor your friend's choice.

Sometimes their preference may shift over time. Someone who once described themselves as "hard of hearing" may later feel more comfortable identifying as "Deaf." This does not mean they are inconsistent; it means their identity is evolving as they gain confidence and community.

It's also important to recognize that different situations may call for different words. What your communication partner tells a friendly barista might be different than what they say to an emergency first responder. With the barista they see regularly, they might say: *"I'm hard of hearing and I need to see your face so I can lipread. If I miss something, saying it again a little slower really helps."* But in a high-stress emergency, they may only have a second to get the point across, so a quick *"I'm deaf"* may be all they can manage.

How people interpret those words also matters. If your friend with hearing loss says "hard of hearing," some people think, "Oh, they can hear me if I just talk louder," which causes frustration if that assumption isn't true. On the other hand, words like "deaf" or "hearing impaired" are often understood to mean there is significant difficulty understanding speech and that accommodations are needed. You might notice your friend choosing "deaf" not because it perfectly describes their identity, but because it gets others to take communication challenges seriously.

Finally, be aware that saying "hard of hearing" can unintentionally shift responsibility onto them, as if it's their job to "try harder" to understand. This misunderstanding can place an unfair emotional and practical burden on your friend.

Ally in Action

- **Mirror language:** Use the same words they use.

- **Respect change:** Adjust as their preferences evolve.

- **Notice context:** Recognize that the words they choose may shift depending on urgency or situation.

Ally Insights

- Do I default to medical or outdated terms without asking what my loved one prefers?

- How do I react when their language choices differ from mine?

- How do I show respect for their evolving identity through the words I use?

In *Becoming Hearing Empowered*, your loved one reflects on labels they prefer in the journal activity called **My Words**.

Ask:

- "What words feel right to you right now?"

- "Are there any you'd prefer I avoid?"

- "Would you like me to help remind others of your preferences?"

By respecting their choices and supporting their voice, you strengthen trust and affirm that their hearing loss, and how they describe it, deserves dignity.

Section 3: Identity

ALLY PERSPECTIVE: WHY THIS MATTERS

For your communication partner, integrating hearing loss into their identity isn't just about wearing devices or asking for captions. It's about reshaping how they see themselves in a world that often stigmatizes difference. This process can be unsettling, because it requires confronting fears of rejection, painful past experiences, and cultural expectations of "normal hearing." Your acceptance helps create the safety they need to move from hiding their hearing loss toward embracing it as a natural, authentic part of who they are.

Integrating Hearing Loss into Identity

For many people, hearing loss is not just a condition. It becomes part of their identity because it significantly shapes how they communicate and interact with the world. Communication is at the heart of relationships, work, and daily life, and hearing loss changes the way those interactions unfold. Whether it means relying on technology, requesting accommodations, or finding new strategies to stay connected, these adjustments become part of how a person lives, and therefore, part of who they are.

Some try to ignore or hide their hearing loss because of stigma or fear of being judged. They avoid telling new friends or coworkers, hoping to "pass" as hearing. Others downplay their devices or refuse to advocate for access in order to avoid calling attention to themselves.

On the other hand, some people eventually reach a place where they embrace hearing loss as an important part of who they are. It doesn't define them completely, but it's an authentic piece of their whole self, like being a parent, an artist, or an athlete.

Integrating hearing loss into identity often brings relief, because the energy once spent hiding or denying is now spent on living openly and fully. But this step is hard-won, requiring self-reflection, support, and often years of experience.

Why This Is Difficult

Including hearing loss in identity is challenging for several reasons. Stigma has long taught people to see hearing devices or accommodations as weaknesses. Fear of rejection, or of being negatively judged, makes disclosure feel risky. Cultural expectations value 'normal hearing,' making difference feel like failure. And personal history may include painful memories of teasing, exclusion, or being misunderstood.

For your communication partner, embracing hearing loss may mean confronting these memories and reshaping the way they see themselves.

- **When hearing loss comes up in conversation**, don't rush past it or change the subject. Let it be mentioned as naturally as any other fact about them.

- **When you introduce them to someone new**, don't preemptively explain their hearing loss for them, unless they've asked you to. Let them decide what to share and when.

- **When you notice something they do well that connects to their experience** (patience, attention to detail, reading body language, persistence), name it. "You always notice when someone's uncomfortable before I do" or "You don't give up easily."

ALLY INSIGHTS

- Do I treat their hearing loss as one part of who they are, or as the defining thing about them?

- Have I ever said or thought "despite their hearing loss" when describing their strengths? What would it mean to say "including their hearing loss" instead?

In *Becoming Hearing Empowered*, your loved one is completing two reflective activities: **I Am…** (where they finish the phrase "I am…" in multiple ways) and **My Identity + My Hearing Loss Identity** (where they place hearing loss alongside five other identity traits in circles). Examples of the journal activities are found at the end of this section.

If they're willing to share, ask: "How did it feel to put hearing loss in the same space as your other traits?"

For some, this feels uncomfortable. Seeing hearing loss given equal weight may challenge old patterns of hiding. For others, it feels affirming. Either response is valid. If they share their circles with you, notice where you fit in their identity map. What does that tell you about your role in their life?

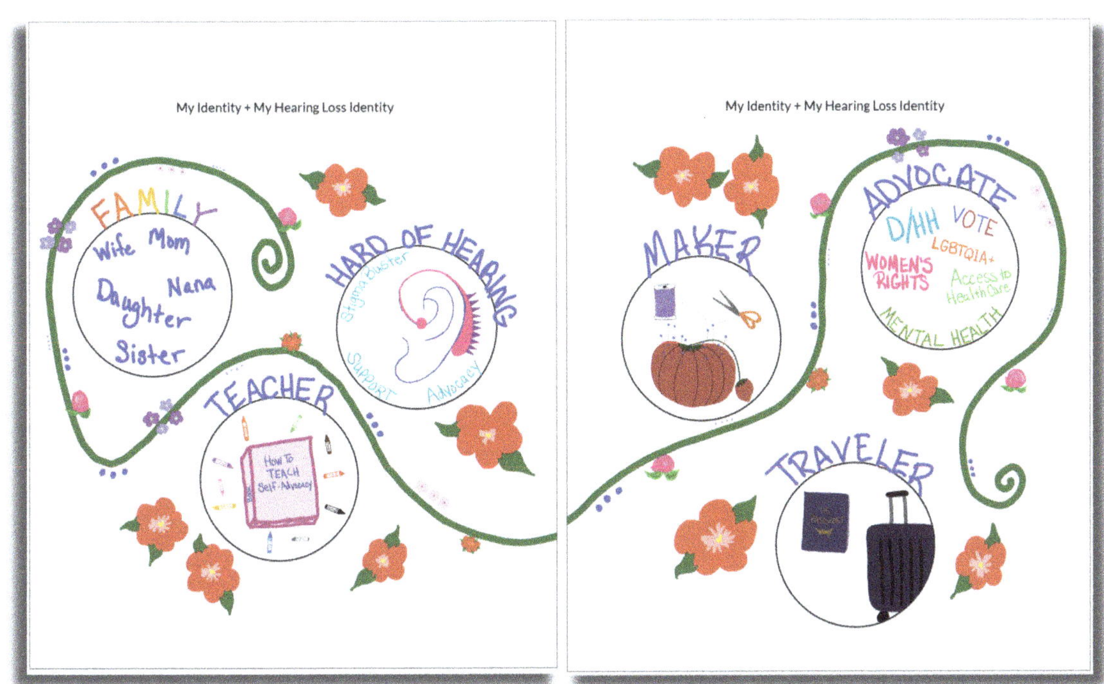

My Identity + My Hearing Loss Identity
FAMILY
Wife Mom
Daughter Nana
Sister
TEACHER
How to TEACH Self-Advocacy
HARD OF HEARING
Stigma Buster
SUPPORT
Advocacy
My Identity + My Hearing Loss Identity
MAKER
ADVOCATE
D/HH VOTE
LGBTQIA+
WOMEN'S RIGHTS
Access to Health Care
MENTAL HEALTH
TRAVELER

Section 4: Community & Introvert vs. Extrovert

Your loved one doesn't have to navigate hearing loss alone, and neither do you. Connecting with others who share similar experiences brings validation, belonging, and practical wisdom that even the most supportive hearing ally cannot fully provide. At the same time, hearing loss shapes how your loved one shows up socially in ways that are easy to misread. An extrovert who withdraws from group conversations isn't becoming antisocial; they're managing an inaccessible environment. An introvert who dominates discussions isn't showing off; they're trying to stay in control of unpredictable communication. Community gives them belonging; your understanding gives them permission to be themselves.

Community

With identity comes community. Hearing loss is isolating because it makes communication difficult, not just for the person with hearing loss, but for everyone trying to stay connected. It's important to understand that your friend with hearing loss is not alone. There are countless others who have faced the same challenges and found strength, pride, and belonging through shared experience. Alongside them, you will find other hearing allies–people that are learning how to communicate and support their person with hearing loss. You will likely find you have much in common and they become your own community.

Let's talk about the words used to define these communities. Communities that include people across all levels of hearing loss, from slight to profound, and that are not defined by a single language (spoken or signed) are often referred to as the **d/Deaf and Hard of Hearing community**, the **hearing loss community**, or, less commonly, the **deaf community** (where "deaf" represents the full continuum of hearing levels).

The **Deaf community** includes people who use sign language and share cultural and linguistic traditions connected to Deaf identity. The **Hard of Hearing community** includes people who use spoken language and generally identify within the hearing world rather than as part of a distinct culture. The **hearing community**, those without hearing disabilities, makes up the dominant culture that primarily communicates through spoken language. However, the hearing community often has less awareness of the challenges and experiences faced by those with hearing loss.

Encouraging your friend to connect with these communities can make a profound difference. Local, state, national, and even international organizations exist to serve people with hearing loss. Getting involved provides belonging, reduces isolation, and offers meaningful relationships with others who truly understand their lived experience, and yours as someone who supports them.

When Personality and Hearing Loss Clash

Extroverts: An extroverted person loves social energy and thrives on group interactions. But with hearing loss, group settings filled with background noise become draining and discouraging. The extroverted person with a hearing loss may withdraw, not because they've become introverted, but because the environment makes participation too exhausting. Outsiders assume they're shy or antisocial, when in reality, they feel shut out or choose a more solitary role simply because they are trying to manage socializing with a hearing loss.

Introverts: An introverted person prefers smaller groups or quiet one-on-one conversations. But the introverted person with hearing loss might feel pressured to take control of the conversation, to steer topics or speak more often, simply to avoid being caught off guard. This looks like they're outgoing, extroverted or even dominating, but really they're trying to manage their anxiety about missing information.

When coping behaviors are mistaken for personality, it creates misunderstanding both inside and outside the relationship. It helps to understand that what looks like "withdrawal" or "disinterest" may actually be self-preservation. Your friend might be an extrovert who feels stifled by the limits hearing loss imposes on group participation; or an introvert who is over engaging and steering the interaction in an attempt to follow complex, fast-paced conversations. Recognizing this helps you identify environments where they can show up as their authentic selves, without exhaustion, frustration, or fear of being left out.

- **Before a social event**, ask: "What would make this easier for you? A quieter corner, sitting near people you know, or a plan to leave early if it gets overwhelming?"

- **When they withdraw at a gathering**, don't assume they're being antisocial. Check in privately: "Do you need a break, or would it help if I stayed close?"

- **When you notice them dominating a conversation**, consider that they might be steering to avoid getting lost, not showing off. Later, ask gently: "Was that easier than trying to follow everyone else?"

- **If they express interest in connecting with others who have hearing loss**, offer support: "Would you like me to look for local support groups with you?" or "Want company if you decide to go?"

- When my loved one seems "off" in social situations (withdrawn, talkative, tense, or checked out), what might they be managing that I can't see?

- Do I describe them to others in ways that might actually be coping behaviors? (For example: "She's so quiet" or "He always takes over conversations.")

In *Becoming Hearing Empowered*, your loved one is completing the activity **Introvert vs. Extrovert**, reflecting on how hearing loss has shaped the way they show up socially, and whether that matches who they really are.

If they're open to sharing, ask: "What kinds of settings make it easiest for you to just... be you?"

This question opens a door to deeper conversation without putting them on the defensive. Listen for contrasts. If they describe places where they feel most like themselves, take note. These are environments to prioritize together. If they mention settings that feel exhausting or forced, that's valuable too. And if they express interest in connecting with others who have hearing loss, explore options without pressure: "Would you want to try it alone first, or would it help if I came along?"

Section 5: Hearing Technology

For many, choosing to wear hearing technology openly is an act of courage. These devices can restore access, ease fatigue, and keep relationships strong, yet stigma often makes people feel embarrassed or "less than" for using them. When you treat devices as normal, valuable, and even stylish, you help reframe them as tools of empowerment and connection, not symbols of weakness.

Hearing technology, whether hearing aids, cochlear implants, bone-anchored hearing aids, or other assistive devices, can be life-changing. These tools provide access to sound, improve communication, and often reduce listening fatigue. But they also carry a heavy weight of stigma.

For generations, hearing aids were designed to be hidden, reinforcing the message that hearing loss was something to be ashamed of. Even today, many people feel reluctant to wear their devices openly because they fear looking old, weak, or "broken." This stigma can deeply affect self-identity.

Reimagining hearing technology as something visible, empowering, and even stylish helps dismantle shame. Just as eyeglasses once carried stigma but are now viewed as fashionable and practical, hearing devices can also be reframed as symbols of strength, resilience, and connection.

ALLY IN ACTION

- **Normalize visibility:** Talk about devices openly, just as you would glasses.

- **Reframe positively:** Emphasize that devices are empowering tools, not signs of weakness.

- **Encourage personalization:** Support them if they want to decorate or customize their devices, like colorful cases, skins, or jewelry.

- How do I feel when my loved one wears their devices openly?

- Do I ever reinforce stigma by treating devices as something to hide?

- How do I help reframe hearing technology as empowering and even stylish?

In *Becoming Hearing Empowered,* your friend with hearing loss completes the journal activities **Visible Hearing Technology & Identity** and **Hearing Technology in a Positive Light.** They are asked to reflect on their feelings about hearing technology; whether they feel embarrassed, neutral, or proud of it. They also consider ways to make their devices more comfortable or stylish.

Ask:

- "How do you feel about your devices being visible?"

- "Do you ever feel pressure to hide them?"

- "Would you like to reimagine them as something expressive, like glasses or jewelry?"

- "Is there a way I could support you, like helping you explore accessories or designs, that might make them feel more like part of your identity?"

By affirming that devices are normal and valuable, you help dismantle stigma and create space for your friend to embrace their technology with pride.

6 | technology & accommodations

I didn't understand the remote microphone until I saw it work.

We were at a noisy restaurant, the kind of place my friend usually avoided. But this time, she handed me a small device and asked me to clip it to my collar.

"Just talk normally," she said.

I did. And for the first time in years, she didn't lean in, didn't furrow her brow, didn't ask me to repeat. She just... listened. And responded. Like it was easy.

"This is amazing. Is everything so much easier now?" I asked.

She shook her head. "This is what it's like when all the technology works, the environment isn't overwhelming, and I'm not already exhausted. It doesn't always line up like this. But, yes! This is so much easier right now!"

I hadn't realized how many things had to go right. I'd thought the hearing aids did all the work. I was just starting to understand how much more there was to it.

Section 1: Find Your Professional

ALLY PERSPECTIVE: WHY THIS MATTERS

Choosing the right professional is just as important as choosing the right device. An audiologist who listens, explains options, and respects your loved one's goals makes the difference between frustration and empowerment. Help by encouraging research, supporting their choices, and making sure they feel heard every step of the way.

Personal hearing technology like hearing aids and cochlear implants can be life-changing, but they're only one part of the bigger picture. Devices are most effective when paired with knowledge, follow-up, and additional accommodations that make daily life accessible. Learning about this process helps you become a more informed partner and a stronger advocate.

Whether your friend is just now considering hearing aids and/or cochlear implants, or they have worn them for years, it is important for them to be informed when it comes to choosing the right technology. In this chapter, we will touch briefly on the basics, but the main focus will be on how your friend becomes an active, empowered self-advocate who digs deeper into the process than simply choosing from the one or two options recommended by their audiologist.

Now, don't get me wrong. The audiologist is the expert in hearing technology, but doing a little research and preparation before the appointment empowers you and your friend to ask more questions and ensure their needs are fully taken into consideration when choosing the best devices.

Step One: Find Your Professional

Hands down, most experienced hearing aid users will recommend that your loved one see an audiologist (Doctor of Audiology–AuD) rather than a hearing care specialist or hearing aid fitting specialist. Audiologists have significantly more expertise, come from accredited educational institutions, and provide much more value in exchange for your loved one's time and money.

Time is a key factor in this process. Purchasing and being fit with new hearing aids or cochlear implant processors is rarely a one- or two-appointment matter. When your loved one purchases hearing devices, a significant portion of the cost often includes professional services, such as follow-up care, technical support, and adjustments, to ensure the devices function effectively for their individual needs. It's important to remember that achieving the best sound in your loved one's everyday listening environments takes time and collaboration. Follow-up visits allow the audiologist to fine-tune the settings, address comfort issues, and help your loved one get the most benefit from their devices.

Many audiologists only fit certain brands of devices. If your loved one has their eye on a specific hearing aid from a specific manufacturer, it's important to find out ahead of time if it will be available at the chosen audiologist's office.

If your loved one needs help finding a good audiologist, check with local organizations and agencies to get recommendations. Or even offer to help with this step if they'd like your support.

Check out **hearingoutloud.net/resources** for tips on how to find an audiologist in your area.

- **Promote professional expertise:** Recommend seeking an audiologist (AuD) who specializes in hearing technology rather than relying on general hearing aid dealers.

- **Value time and follow-up:** Remind your communication partner that multiple fittings and adjustments are normal, and worth it for the best results.

- **Share the load:** Offer to help with contacting audiology offices if they'd find that helpful, without taking control.

ALLY INSIGHTS

- Do I know the difference between audiologists, ENTs, and hearing specialists?

- How do I support my friend with hearing loss in finding a professional who respects their needs?

- How do I be a partner in this process without taking over?

In *Becoming Hearing Empowered*, your friend's journal activity is a chart titled, **Questions for Potential Audiologists**. If they do not yet have a trusted professional, choosing the right audiologist shapes how confident and supported they feel throughout their hearing care experience. Be an active partner by helping them think through what matters most, not by deciding for them, but by ensuring they have the information they need to choose wisely.

Ask if they'd like your help researching or comparing options. Look up reviews together, call offices to clarify details, or help organize notes from the question chart.

Section 2: Do Your Homework

ALLY PERSPECTIVE: WHY THIS MATTERS

This section is full of technical details—brands, batteries, features, and performance levels—that may not seem directly relevant to you. But your knowledge makes a difference. When you understand the options, you become a stronger partner and a more effective advocate. You help your loved one ask better questions, notice tradeoffs, and feel less alone in navigating complex decisions.

Once your friend with hearing loss has found an audiologist and has scheduled an appointment, it's time for them to begin researching. If they are considering hearing aids or cochlear implants for the very first time, or if they are an experienced user looking for replacement or upgraded devices, the entire process can feel overwhelming. Encourage them to dedicate time to familiarize themselves with the different devices available and learn about the multitude of features.

Audiologists have a finite amount of time with each patient. They want people to experience the maximum benefit of the devices they purchase. For new users, they recognize that the amount of information is overwhelming, so they often try to simplify.

If your friend is new to hearing loss and new to wearing hearing aids, all of this can leave their head spinning. Only they know what they really need in a hearing device. Their audiologist will spend time asking about the different environments where they struggle, but likely won't go into depth. That's why preparation matters.

Learning how to care for hearing aids, change batteries, switch programs, and more takes time and an adjustment period. This is why, based on the hearing test and a brief interview, audiologists often recommend one or two options they feel will give someone the best chance at becoming a successful hearing device user. If your friend hasn't researched brands and features of the models suggested, they miss opportunities to find the best devices for their lifestyle.

Power Options

Most hearing aids and cochlear implant processors come with a choice of power options, including rechargeable lithium-ion batteries and disposable zinc-air batteries.

Rechargeable options are convenient if your loved one is conscientious about sticking to a routine of placing devices on the charger each night. They typically last about 12 hours on a single charge, even with Bluetooth streaming, and battery life continues to improve as new models are released. Rechargeables allow them to go about their day without random low battery warnings and without changing batteries in the middle of the day. Generally, rechargeable options require a slightly larger device.

One drawback of rechargeable devices is that if the battery runs low before your loved one's day is over, they'll need to remove the devices to recharge them. Since many people wear their hearing aids longer than 12 hours, this could mean being without sound support while the batteries recharge. If the batteries stop charging properly, the audiologist may need to send the devices to the manufacturer for repair or replacement, which could leave your loved one without them for a week or more. In some cases, audiologists provide loaner devices to use during that time.

Disposable batteries offer an immediate remedy if power runs out: simply change them and they're good to go. There's no need to wait for a recharge, making them ideal for long days, travel, or unpredictable schedules. If your loved one carries a pack of batteries with them, it reduces worries about being caught without sound. Disposable batteries also come in various sizes, allowing for smaller devices.

There are some tradeoffs. Disposable batteries require ongoing purchases, which add up over time. They also demand a bit of planning: keeping spares on hand, monitoring battery life, and remembering to restock. Changing the tiny batteries requires some dexterity, which is challenging for those with vision or fine motor difficulties. And for environmentally conscious users, the waste from discarded batteries is a consideration. Many pharmacies and grocery stores carry hearing aid batteries, but availability varies, so planning ahead matters.

Brands

There are about six major brands of hearing aids in North America: Sonova (Phonak, Unitron), ReSound, Siemens (Signia, Rexton), Starkey, Widex, and Oticon. There are three cochlear implant manufacturers: Cochlear, Med-El, and Advanced Bionics.

Cochlear implant users must stick with the brand they were implanted with, though processors are updated with new styles and features. Hearing aid users have greater flexibility between brands; however, not all audiologists carry all brands. If your friend is interested in a certain brand or model, it's important to check with the audiologist's office.

Most brands also carry accessories. If your communication partner is interested in using a specific accessory, suggest they ask whether that brand is supported. For example, Phonak's Roger microphones are remote microphones that greatly improve speech understanding in noise and at a distance. While these work with other manufacturers, they work seamlessly with Phonak aids because the receivers are programmed directly into the devices.

Check out **hearingoutloud.net/resources** for links to suppliers of hearing aids and cochlear implants.

Styles, Features & Performance Levels

Hearing aids and cochlear implants come in many styles. Depending on how your loved one feels about wearing visible hearing technology, encourage them to consider more than just invisibility when choosing. While some prefer devices that are hidden, visible devices may sometimes reduce the constant need to self-disclose their hearing loss.

It's also important to understand that smaller, more discreet devices sacrifice certain features. If the primary goal is to hear and understand better in multiple environments, prioritizing performance over invisibility leads to more satisfying results.

Hearing devices come with many different features, such as Bluetooth connectivity, telecoils, rechargeable batteries, streaming options, and apps that let the user control settings from a phone. They're also available at different performance levels, basic, standard, advanced, and premium, usually linked to price and technology. Premium models include extra programs like *speech in loud noise* or *comfort in echo* that make certain listening situations easier. Lower levels have fewer of these features, and warranty coverage also varies depending on the model.

Help your loved one by encouraging them to research brand websites, look at the feature charts, and note the performance levels. Many manufacturers provide side-by-side comparisons that make options easier to understand.

T-Coil or Telecoil

A telecoil allows a hearing aid to connect directly with compatible phones and induction loop systems. Many public places: churches, theaters, meeting halls, have loops installed. While many hearing aids include a telecoil, this feature often must be specifically requested from the audiologist.

Encourage your friend to ask about it, especially if they attend public events where loops are common.

Auracast

Auracast is an emerging technology designed to improve audio accessibility not only for people with hearing loss but for the general population. It allows high-quality audio to be broadcast from sources like public address systems or personal devices directly to hearing aids, cochlear implants, earbuds, or headphones via Bluetooth.

Unlike traditional Bluetooth, Auracast supports multiple simultaneous streams, similar to selecting a Wi-Fi network. For example, airports could broadcast gate announcements directly into devices, or theaters could provide multiple audio streams (different languages, or audio description for blind patrons).

This technology is still being rolled out. At the time of publication (Spring 2026), most hearing devices were not yet Auracast ready. Encourage your friend with hearing loss to ask their audiologist about future compatibility. In the meantime, many venues still rely on telecoil loop systems, so having that feature remains important.

Not a Perfect Fix

Hearing aids and cochlear implant processors usually help people hear better than without them, but they cannot replicate natural hearing. Even with major technological advances, your loved one may still have difficulty understanding speech in noisy environments. It's also important to remember that these devices take time to adjust to. A person who has lived without sound for a while may feel overwhelmed when new devices suddenly make background noises, like rustling papers or footsteps, seem loud or distracting. This adjustment period is normal and improves with time, support, and patience. For hearing people, this is hard to grasp, since glasses often restore vision to crystal clarity. Hearing devices don't work that way. They improve access, but they don't remove all barriers. Accessories and assistive technologies help, but understanding, patience, and realistic expectations are essential.

- **Encourage preparation:** Support your friend in researching brands, features, and styles before the appointment.

- **Break it down:** Offer to help compare key differences (rechargeable vs. disposable, brand A vs. brand B) without overwhelming them.

- **Keep expectations realistic:** Remind both of you that hearing devices improve access, but they don't "fix" hearing the way glasses often "fix" vision.

- **Respect pacing:** If your friend doesn't want help right now, step back. Let them set the pace for how much information to take in.

ALLY INSIGHTS

- How comfortable am I with learning technical information about hearing devices?

- Do I tend to dismiss or downplay these details as "not important," or do I see how they matter to my loved one's daily life?

- How do I use what I learn to make my support practical, without taking over their choices?

While there isn't a formal journal activity in this section of *Becoming Hearing Empowered*, your loved one may take notes or make lists about device features and brand options. Connect by asking:

- "What features are you most interested in? Things like rechargeable or telecoils?"

- "Would it help if I looked up some brand comparisons with you?"

- "Do you want me to keep track of the pros and cons so you don't have to juggle it all in your head?"

Even if they'd rather do the research on their own, knowing that you respect the process, and that you're willing to listen or help if asked, makes them feel less alone in the decision-making.

Section 3: Accessories, Cost, & Preparing for the Audiology Appointment

ALLY PERSPECTIVE: WHY THIS MATTERS

The world of accessories, features, and costs feels overwhelming. Learning about these tools makes you an informed partner. It helps you understand the real-life challenges your loved one faces and the options available to support them. Your awareness allows you to encourage realistic decisions, advocate during appointments, and provide reassurance when financial considerations feel discouraging.

ACCESSORIES

There are many accessories available today that can enhance the function of your friend's hearing aids or cochlear implant processors.

Remote Control

The ability to control hearing devices remotely, using a handheld remote or an app on a smartphone, makes it easier to adjust programs or volume without fiddling with tiny buttons. These adjustments change the direction of microphones, focusing on the person speaking in front instead of noise behind, or adjust volume in one or both ears.

Remote Microphones

Hearing devices are usually equipped with multiple microphones at ear level, but these work best when the sound source is close and background noise is limited. In situations like a presentation 15 feet away or a noisy restaurant, built-in microphones don't perform well enough.

Remote microphones solve this problem. They clip on a shirt, can be placed on a table, or held in "interview mode" to pick up voices at a distance and send the sound directly to the user's ears. Some use digital/FM signals (like Phonak's Roger system), while others use Bluetooth (mini-mic, partner mic, multi-mic). DM/FM mics are usually more expensive but can provide stronger performance.

For many, these microphones are game changers, making restaurants, sporting events, car rides, and shopping trips enjoyable again.

TV Connector

Most manufacturers offer TV connectors that stream sound directly from the television to the hearing devices. These accessories enhance sound clarity for the person wearing the devices while still allowing others in the room to listen to the TV as they normally would.

Streamers

Using Bluetooth, streamers clip to a shirt or lanyard and allow sound from phones, laptops, or tablets to stream directly into devices. Increasingly, new hearing aids and processors have Bluetooth built in, eliminating the need for a streamer.

A WORD ABOUT COST

Hearing technology is expensive, and most insurance companies do not cover hearing aids for adults. The decision to purchase technology is a major one, but the cost must be weighed against quality of life.

For people who don't use sign language, hearing and speaking are often their primary way of connecting with loved ones, colleagues, and their communities. Hearing better allows them to once again enjoy conversations, television, podcasts, plays, movies, audiobooks, and music.

Most of the time, the price of hearing aids includes more than just the devices. Costs are usually bundled with the hearing test, consultation, initial fitting, follow-up adjustments, cleanings, and a warranty that lasts 1–3 years. Purchased separately, these services would add thousands of dollars.

There are funding options, too. State Vocational Rehabilitation agencies may help if devices are needed for work or school. Other local agencies and nonprofits may provide support as well.

Check out **hearingoutloud.net/resources** for helpful links to major agencies and resources.

Cost Comparisons

- Two premium Bluetooth hearing aids + DM microphone + bundled services cost ~$8,000. Over 7 years, worn 12 hours per day, this averages to about $0.27 per hour, or $3.24 per day, the price of a cup of coffee.

- Two mid-level performance hearing aids + partner mic + bundled services cost ~$6,000. Over 7 years, that's about $0.20 per hour, or $2.34 per day.

Framed this way, the cost becomes less about a one-time sticker shock and more about daily value for restored connection and participation in life.

PREPARING FOR THE AUDIOLOGY APPOINTMENT

Because audiologists have limited appointment time, it's important for your friend with hearing loss to prepare in advance. Encourage them to identify what matters most:

- What environments are hardest (restaurants, family dinners, work meetings)?

- What features are priorities (Bluetooth, telecoil, rechargeables)?

- What accessories could make a difference (remote mic, TV connector)?

Bringing this list to the appointment ensures the audiologist considers their true needs, not just the basics.

- **Before the appointment, ask:** "Would it help if I looked up remote microphones or TV connectors for the brands you're considering?"

- **When cost comes up**, resist the urge to say "that's too expensive" or "you don't need the premium version." Instead, help reframe: "What's it worth to you to hear better at family dinners? At work? Watching movies together?"

- **At the appointment**, sit slightly behind them, not between them and the audiologist. Take notes if they ask. Speak up only if they invite you to, or if the audiologist directs a question to you.

- **If they seem overwhelmed by choices**, offer to organize, not decide. "Want me to make a comparison chart of the three options so you can think it over tonight?"

- When it comes to their hearing technology, do I see myself as a helper or a decision-maker? What's the difference?

- Have I ever pushed my opinion about what they should buy, how much they should spend, or which features matter most? What was driving that?

In *Becoming Hearing Empowered*, your loved one works through the activity **Preparing for Your Audiology Appointment**. They reflect on their feelings, note their health history and daily challenges, and mark which features matter most to them.

You've likely noticed patterns they don't see themselves—observations that could help the audiologist understand their real-world challenges. Before offering, ask: "Would it be helpful if I shared some things I've noticed, or would you rather go through this on your own?"

This respects their autonomy while making clear you're available. If they say no, honor that without taking offense. If they say yes, share observations as information, not complaints. For example:

- "I've noticed you often ask for repeats in group conversations."

- "Sometimes you don't seem to hear the microwave alarm or the doorbell."

- "When we're in the car, it seems harder for you to follow what I'm saying."

Section 4: Feedback & Follow-Up

The trial period is more than just testing new devices. It's when your loved one learns how the technology fits into daily life and whether adjustments are needed. Your encouragement, patience, and willingness to listen help them feel safe giving honest feedback, which is essential for getting the best possible results. By supporting persistence through follow-ups, you reinforce that their comfort and access are worth the effort.

When your friend receives new devices, there is usually a trial period (often 30 days) with a money-back guarantee, often minus a small fee. This time is crucial for them to get the most out of the investment.

Encourage your friend to wear their devices regularly, ideally 10–12 hours a day, seven days a week. If they've never worn hearing aids before, their brain will need time to recalibrate and adjust to hearing sounds they haven't heard in years. Consistent use gives the best chance of becoming accustomed to the devices and provides plenty of opportunities to judge how effective they are in different listening situations.

Hearing aids and cochlear implant processors are computer-programmable. Before the first fitting, the audiologist sets them using their best guess for balanced sound quality. But those settings are adjustable based on feedback. This is where your friend's detailed input becomes invaluable.

Encourage them to be specific:

- In which situations do they notice improvement compared to their old devices or to no devices at all?

- Which situations are still difficult?

- How does sound quality change when using different programs?

- How do music or phone calls sound when streamed directly?

- What, if anything, would they change?

If your friend is unhappy with certain settings or listening environments, reassure them that many adjustments are possible. Remind them it's normal to need follow-up visits, and that they deserve to keep going back until the settings feel right.

Things to Pay Attention to During the Trial Period

As your friend tries new devices, encourage them to keep track of the situations where the devices worked well, the times when they still struggled, how different listening environments felt (restaurants, meetings, car rides, concerts), the sound quality of streaming calls, TV, or music, any comfort issues with fit or wearing devices all day, and specific questions or frustrations they'd like to bring back to the audiologist. This information helps the audiologist make precise adjustments instead of guessing.

- **Encourage consistency:** Gently remind your loved one to wear their devices every day during the trial.

- **Prompt observations:** Ask if they'd like you to check in at the end of the day to talk about what worked and what didn't.

- **Validate feedback:** Remind them it's okay to be "picky." Feedback isn't complaining; it's how the devices get fine-tuned.

- **Support persistence:** Encourage them to attend as many follow-up appointments as needed.

ALLY INSIGHTS

- Do I understand that device fitting is a process, not a one-time event?

- How do I help my loved one feel comfortable giving detailed, honest feedback without minimizing their concerns?

- Am I patient enough to support multiple follow-ups if adjustments are needed?

In *Becoming Hearing Empowered,* your loved one is encouraged to complete a **21-Day Feedback Diary** as part of the trial period process. The form includes space for: Date, Hours worn, Listening situations, Positives, Negatives, Questions for the audiologist

Ask:

- "Do you want me to add what I notice too, for example, times you ask for repeats, or when you miss alarms or alerts?"

- "Do you want me to come with you to the follow-up appointment, just to support you or to help make sure your notes are shared?"

By respecting their process and offering support, you help ensure they get the full benefit of the trial period.

Section 5: Accommodations & Assistive Technology

ALLY PERSPECTIVE: WHY THIS MATTERS

Personal hearing technology like hearing aids and cochlear implants is only part of the picture. Many people with hearing loss also rely on accommodations and assistive devices to access daily life fully, at work, in school, at home, and in the community. Learning about these tools helps you understand that your loved one's needs don't stop with the audiologist's office. Encourage them to explore resources, help advocate for accommodations, and be ready to back them up when systems fail to provide access.

In addition to personal hearing technology such as hearing aids and cochlear implants, there are a wide variety of accommodations and other assistive technology devices available to help your friend with hearing loss in their day-to-day life.

Captioning

Captions are running text that displays spoken words in visual form. **Closed captioning** refers to on-screen text that appears only when the captioning feature is turned on or when using a special viewing device. The captions are "closed" to the general audience, meaning they aren't visible to everyone; only to those who choose to activate them or view them on a personal device. **Open captioning** is text that is displayed on the screen for the general viewing audience. It is often "burned" into the original video, or in the case of a movie theater, the captions are displayed directly on the screen for every moviegoer to see.

Automated captions, or computer-generated captions, are captions that use voice recognition technology to translate the spoken word to text. While not 100% accurate, this technology has come a long way and is often a great option in a pinch. **Live captions**, or real-time captioning, also referred to as **CART** (Communication Access Realtime Translation), are captions that are provided using a human to translate spoken word to text. These are the most accurate and reliable form of captions for in-person and virtual meetings. In order to be Americans with Disability Act (ADA)-compliant, live captioning is required versus computer-generated captions. This doesn't require the captioner to physically be in the room; they can work virtually if the situation provides high-quality audio. In some situations, your friend can request the transcript for reference instead of taking notes. This is not always allowed, so it's best to ask ahead of time.

Television: Your friend likely already uses captions when watching television. If not, you can encourage them to try. Captions are usually turned on in the settings section of the TV. The option is under the "Accessibility," "Audio," or "Display" menu. The caption display settings, including color and size, are also changed there. It takes a little time to get used to them, but once they try, many people are surprised by how much more they enjoy watching their favorite shows.

Movie theaters: Most movie theaters offer captioning devices that are used right at the seat. They attach in the drink cup holder, and newer versions are displayed using special glasses. Not all movies provide a captioning file, so not every film will have this option. It's always good to check ahead of time. If your friend has never used them before, they usually need to request them at the ticket counter.

Live performances: Many live performances, such as Broadway plays, have real-time captioning available. Ask when purchasing tickets.

Work or school: If your friend requires captions in order to fully access auditory information at school or at work, real-time captioning is an accommodation they may have a right to under the Americans with Disabilities Act. The process to request them depends on the situation. In a university, they contact the office that provides support to students with disabilities and make a request through them. At work, they contact HR or speak directly with a supervisor. In Chapter Seven: *People and Places*, you'll learn more about how to confidently have these conversations.

Speaking on the phone: There are two options for captions while speaking on the phone. Your friend with hearing loss can try apps or accessibility settings in their smartphone that provide computer-generated captions. Another option, using any kind of phone (landline, business phone, cell phone, or smartphone), is a free live captioning service with a live person providing transcription of the conversation. These services are provided free for people with hearing loss or speech disabilities because they're certified by the FCC (Federal Communications Commission) and receive funding from the TRS (Telecommunications Relay Service) fund. There are also landline phones with captioning screens built in for use with real-time caption services. Funding is often available for telecommunications equipment. Check with your local disability resource office.

Home and other social settings: If your friend has a smartphone or tablet, an automated captioning app can provide captions anywhere. As long as there's decent sound quality, they flip on the captioning app and hold it next to the person talking. You'll be surprised how accurate it is.

Check out **hearingoutloud.net/resources** for captioning resources.

Assistive Listening Devices and FM/DM Systems

FM listening systems, and the newer DM listening systems, work in conjunction with hearing aids and cochlear implants (see features and accessories in the previous section of this chapter: *Personal Hearing Technology*). These systems also work with standalone receivers, such as headphones or earpieces provided at the venue. They are generally available at movie theaters, live performance venues, and churches and are located at the ticket or information desks.

Induction Loops

In some public places, such as churches, meeting halls, and live performance theaters, induction loops are installed to send the audio signal from the venue's sound system directly to hearing aids using their T-coil, or telecoil, setting. This can enhance your loved one's ability to hear and understand what's being said. Not all hearing aids are equipped with T-coils, so this is something to add to their list when seeing an audiologist for new devices.

The telecoil permits coupling of the personal hearing aid to sources of electromagnetic energy, such as a hearing aid compatible telephone or an induction loop. The induction loop provides a magnetic, wireless signal that is picked up by hearing devices with telecoils. When hearing aid users are inside the loop and their T-coil setting is activated, any conversation being broadcast on the facility's audio system, such as a church sermon or stage performance, is sent directly to the telecoil in their hearing device. This feature not only extends the listening range of hearing devices, it also eliminates unwanted background noise to increase listening comprehension and enjoyment. Ask at the information desk or look for this symbol to find out if a hearing loop is installed.

Seating

Preferential seating provides better access simply by changing where your friend sits. In a lecture or presentation setting, most people with hearing loss prefer to sit toward the front, but not the very front row. This allows better visual access to the speaker's face and reduces the distance sound must travel. Sitting in the second or third row provides better visual access to others in the room, allowing the person with hearing loss to use facial expressions and body language to fill in any missed information.

In small groups, your friend might ask to move to a quieter location or for everyone to sit in a circle to make lipreading easier. If your friend has unilateral hearing loss (hearing loss in one ear) or better hearing in one ear than the other, adjusting seating to favor the better side is always helpful. In lecture halls, the second or third row with the better ear toward the speaker often works best.

In noisy environments, such as restaurants, seating choice is key. Tables closer to the bar or kitchen will have more background noise. Look for overhead speakers playing music and avoid sitting beneath them. Booths or tables near a wall usually provide quieter conditions. In Chapter Seven: *People and Places*, you'll learn how to analyze frequent locations to optimize access.

Video Calling Apps

For some people, it's easier to use video calling apps like FaceTime, Zoom, or Google Meet.

Seeing facial expressions, lips, and gestures helps with understanding, compared to voice calls alone. People who use sign language rely on video calling apps to communicate directly with other signers.

Video Relay

Videophones are used to make phone calls in American Sign Language (ASL). Video Relay Services (VRS) provide ASL interpreters to interpret calls between ASL and English (or other spoken languages depending on the vendor).

Notetakers

If your loved one attends a class or important work training session and needs to take notes, using a notetaker allows them to maintain visual attention to the speaker and benefit from visual cues such as gestures and facial expressions. If they set this up themselves, they should ask someone they trust to take thorough notes. If attending a university course, the office for students with disabilities usually arranges this accommodation.

If your loved one uses a captioning service as an accommodation, they can also ask if they're allowed to keep the transcript for future reference.

Alert Signal Devices

There are a variety of devices that can alert your friend with hearing loss to important sounds in the home or environment. These use visual signals (flashing lights) or tactile signals (vibration). Alarm clocks include a bed shaker that goes under the pillow or mattress. Other devices alert to a baby cry, carbon monoxide alarm, smoke alarm, doorbell, telephone ring, or severe weather.

Local disability resource offices help locate vendors. Smartphones and smartwatches also provide visual and tactile alerts, and timer functions can substitute for appliance timers (oven, microwave, dryer).

Check out **hearingoutloud.net/resources** for links to alert device vendors.

Hearing Dogs

Hearing service dogs are specially trained to alert their partners to important sounds by making physical contact, such as pawing, nudging, or jumping, and then leading them toward the source of the sound. While some pets naturally respond to noises their owners can't hear, certified hearing service dogs receive specialized training to recognize specific sounds, like alarms, doorbells, or someone calling their name, and to respond appropriately both at home and in public settings.

Check out **hearingoutloud.net/resources** for a list of reputable facilities for hearing service dogs.

- **Learn together:** Explore accommodations and apps so you can help set them up or troubleshoot.

- **Normalize accommodations:** Treat captions, loops, and assistive devices as standard, not as "special treatment."

- **Support advocacy:** Offer to help request captions or seating changes when your loved one doesn't want to navigate it alone.

- **Share observations:** Notice when your loved one struggles (i.e., missing alarms or conversation). Bring it up gently as a reason to try new tools.

ALLY INSIGHTS

- Do I view accommodations as optional extras, or as essential for my friend's full participation?

- How comfortable am I with helping them request or set up accommodations?

- In what ways do I model acceptance of these tools so my friend feels less stigma when using them?

In *Becoming Hearing Empowered,* your communication partner completes the journal activity called **Accommodations & Assistive Technology**. They are asked if they have accommodations or assistive technology ideas that they haven't tried yet and to create an action plan to do so. The activity prompts them to think about:

- What accommodations or technology could help that they haven't tried yet?

- Why haven't they tried it yet? (Cost, access, or lack of assertiveness?)

- Who do they need to talk to in order to request or set up the accommodation?

- Where do they find new devices or technology?

- Do they need financial assistance to obtain it?

Support this process by asking:

- "Would you like to share which accommodations you think could help but you haven't tried yet?"

- "Do you want to brainstorm together who you'd need to talk to or how to find the device?"

- "Would it help if I looked up funding or local resources with you?"

By participating in this activity, you encourage your loved one to move from reflection into action. You also show that you're willing to stand beside them in trying new strategies, not pushing, but offering backup and encouragement.

It was my idea to sit at the big table with everyone else. "It'll be fun," I said. "You'll be fine."

By the main course, my father had stopped trying. The restaurant was loud, people were talking over each other, and he was sitting at the far end—too far from anyone to lipread, too polite to ask people to repeat themselves.

I watched him nod and smile at nothing. I watched him push food around his plate. I watched him disappear into himself while I laughed at jokes he couldn't hear.

In the car, he didn't say anything. He didn't have to. I'd chosen that table. I'd said he'd be fine. I hadn't thought about what "fine" actually required; or whose job it was to make it possible.

Section 1: People

Talking about hearing loss or asking for support isn't always easy. Your loved one might worry about how people will react or feel unsure about when to bring it up. When you understand that this takes courage, you offer gentle reassurance and patience. Knowing you "get it" helps them feel more comfortable being open with others too.

In Chapter 5: *Identity & Self-Love,* your loved one reflected on how hearing loss is part of their identity and practiced self-acceptance. That foundation is important here. When interacting with people and navigating different places, self-acceptance empowers them to disclose their hearing loss, develop assertiveness skills, and stand up for what they need. Each of these steps strengthens confidence and self-esteem.

You play a vital role in this process. The way you respond to communication breakdowns, support disclosure, and help advocate for accommodations all contribute to whether your loved one feels shame, or pride, about their hearing loss.

Hearing loss doesn't just affect one person. It affects communication between people, in every setting, every day. This chapter explores how relationships, environments, and communication habits shape your loved one's experience, and how you play an active role in making those interactions more respectful, inclusive, and empowering.

Hearing Loss is Communication Loss

Hearing loss is unique among disabilities because it directly affects communication between two or more people. This means your friend's hearing loss is not just their problem. Successful communication requires effort on both sides.

When communication breaks down, your friend faces a choice: to pretend they understood, or to disclose their hearing loss and ask for support. Disclosure can feel vulnerable, but it also gives others, including you, the opportunity to step up and do your part.

Remind yourself that hearing loss is really communication loss. When your friend struggles to understand, it is not a personal failure or a lack of effort. It is a shared responsibility that requires adjustments from both partners in the conversation.

No Need to Apologize

Having a hearing loss is simply a fact of your communication partner's life. They didn't ask for it, they didn't do anything to deserve it, and they didn't wake up one day looking for it. It just is. Yet it's incredibly common for people with hearing loss to say "I'm sorry," "pardon me," or "excuse me," because it feels like the polite thing to do. The people they interact with each day, many of whom don't know anyone with hearing loss, often carry countless misconceptions about it. If others see their hearing aids or cochlear implant processors, they may wrongly assume those devices have "fixed" the problem, especially if your communication partner speaks clearly. When your partner apologizes after missing something, it unintentionally reinforces the misconception that they alone are responsible for keeping up, as if they didn't listen closely enough or didn't try hard enough to understand.

Help shift that dynamic. Gently remind them, and others, that communication is a shared effort, not a solo task. There are many ways to address breakdowns with confidence, which we'll explore in this chapter, but one thing is certain, it's an imperfect situation that's not their fault, so there's no need for them to apologize.

- **Reframe responsibility:** Remind yourself that hearing loss is communication loss, and both partners must adapt.

- **Support disclosure:** Encourage your loved one when they explain their needs instead of pretending to understand.

- **Discourage apologies:** Reinforce that asking for repeats or clarification is not something to be sorry for.

- **Model adjustments:** When others are present, demonstrate patience, repetition, or rephrasing to normalize it.

- How do I respond when my loved one shares their hearing loss or asks for support?

- Have I noticed them apologizing when communication breaks down, and how do I react?

- Do I see communication as a shared effort, or do I assume it's their responsibility to keep up?

In *Becoming Hearing Empowered,* your friend with hearing loss completes the activity **Who Are My People?** They draw a diagram with concentric circles to map out the people in their life:

- **Inner circle:** Closest family and friends; the people they spend the most time with socially.

- **Second circle:** People they see frequently but not intimately: coworkers, neighbors, friends of friends.

- **Third circle:** Professionals they interact with regularly: doctors, teachers, pharmacists, bosses.

- **Outer circle:** Strangers or acquaintances they occasionally interact with: grocery clerks, bus drivers, repair technicians.

This diagram helps your friend think about where communication challenges may arise and which relationships require different approaches to self-disclosure or accommodations.

Ask:

- "Would you like to share your Who Are My People? diagram with me?"

- "How do I support you in talking with people in your outer circles, like a server, cashier, or bus driver, so it feels less stressful?"

Also reflect on your own role in the diagram. Where do you fit, and how do you best support communication in that space? This activity is a chance for both of you to better understand the people who shape daily interactions and how hearing loss plays a role in each circle.

Section 2: Self-Disclosure

Hearing loss is often invisible, especially if devices aren't obvious, so your loved one may need to disclose their hearing loss again and again in different situations. This can be exhausting, but it's also the only way they can reliably get the access and accommodations they need. Understanding the different ways self-disclosure works will help you recognize the effort your loved one is putting in, respect their choices in how they disclose, and know when to step in with support.

Self-Disclosure

Because hearing loss is an invisible disability, your friend must often tell others about it in order to receive equal access and fully participate in conversations. There are multiple ways they might self-disclose, and the approach depends on who they are speaking with and the situation.

Nonverbal Self-Disclosure

Think of disabilities that require an aid, making the disability instantly apparent, such as the use of a wheelchair or white cane. In these cases, self-disclosure isn't immediately necessary, and most people instinctively know how to provide basic accommodations, like stepping out of the way or offering assistance. Your friend's hearing technology (hearing aids or cochlear implant processors) might be easily visible, and a simple finger point to them can clue others in. Unfortunately, people don't always recognize what they're pointing to. There is a wide variety of electronics people wear on their ears, so a hearing aid or cochlear implant may not clearly indicate hearing loss.

Tattoos are another form of nonverbal self-disclosure and can reinforce pride in identity. A popular one is the "mute" symbol placed behind an ear.

Many people, especially during the pandemic, chose to wear a button or article of clothing stating "I have hearing loss" or indicating that they read lips or use sign language. This kind of nonverbal self-disclosure can be effective in occupational settings where your friend encounters many strangers, such as a store clerk or restaurant server. When directly communicating with many people, a quick reference to a button or T-shirt that says "hard of hearing," "deaf," or "I read lips" can make interactions a little smoother. A quick search on Etsy.com will turn up a variety of products that include this kind of personalization. A word of caution: in certain locations or situations (like a walking path or bus station), wearing something that identifies a person as unable to hear may put them in a vulnerable position.

Brief Self-Disclosure

A brief disclosure is a short phrase meant to get the most essential information across quickly, usually to people in the outermost circle, such as strangers. Your loved one may have practiced this in their journal activity "My Words." These are the words they can use to describe their hearing loss in a way that feels natural to them.

Technical Self-Disclosure

A technical disclosure includes more detailed information about the specific kind of hearing loss a person has. It may reference what they learned about ear anatomy and audiograms, details like stability, laterality, degree, and configuration of their hearing loss. They might also mention surgeries, or the types of hearing technology they've used. This kind of disclosure is most often used when speaking with professionals who have background knowledge of hearing loss, such as audiologists, speech pathologists, or other individuals with hearing loss.

Expanded Self-Disclosure

More than a brief disclosure, an expanded disclosure provides information about how a person functionally hears: how their hearing technology works, which sounds are most difficult, and how background noise or an obstructed view of the speaker's mouth can interfere with understanding speech. Your friend with hearing loss might use this type of disclosure with people in their second circle: those they see frequently, such as coworkers, neighbors, and friends. These individuals may already know about the hearing loss, but they may benefit from a better understanding of how it impacts them day to day.

Emotional Self-Disclosure

An emotional disclosure includes the same information as an expanded disclosure, but also adds thoughts, feelings, preferences, and hopes about how hearing loss impacts life emotionally. This is a longer, more personal conversation where your loved one shares the struggles they've experienced, their feelings about stigma, and their path from "impairment" to empowerment. The emotional self-disclosure is meant for the closest people in their life; people like you.

It's important to recognize the trust and vulnerability this kind of sharing requires. Listening with empathy, asking questions, and showing understanding helps your loved one feel truly seen and supported.

It's worth taking time to think about how your loved one discloses their hearing loss and how you can respond in ways that reinforce their confidence and self-acceptance. Their approach will vary depending on who they're speaking with, and your understanding can make each kind of disclosure a little easier.

ALLY IN ACTION

- **Validate the effort:** Recognize how much energy repeated self-disclosure requires.

- **Respect boundaries:** Support their choice of when and how to disclose.

- **Back them up:** If someone dismisses or misunderstands their disclosure, reinforce it respectfully.

- **Encourage deeper sharing:** With trust, invite emotional disclosure to better understand their feelings.

- How do I react when my loved one discloses their hearing loss? Do I show support or discomfort?

- Do I sometimes assume they should "just tell people" without considering the emotional labor involved?

- How do I be a safe person for emotional disclosure, not just technical details?

In *Becoming Hearing Empowered,* your friend with hearing loss builds a **Self-Disclosure Kit**. They'll:

- **Draft** versions of each disclosure type (nonverbal, brief, technical, expanded, emotional).

- **Match** drafts to specific settings/people (i.e., server, coworker, new doctor, close friend).

- **Refine & rehearse:** writing the exact words, practicing them, and visualizing saying them confidently.

How you can support:

- "Would you like to brainstorm scripts together for each circle: strangers, coworkers, close friends?"

- "Want to role-play a few quick scenarios (i.e., ordering at a restaurant, meeting a new provider) so the words feel natural?"

- "Are there safety contexts where you'd rather not disclose?"

- "In real life, do you want me to back you up after you disclose (i.e., 'We'll slow down and face you when we talk'), or stay quiet unless you ask?"

Section 3: Teaching People How to Treat Them

Every interaction your loved one has with someone is a chance to shape how they are treated. Over time, patterns develop, some helpful, some frustrating. You play a critical role in reinforcing positive patterns and gently disrupting negative ones. The way you respond either increases their confidence or adds to the burden they already feel.

How It Works

Assertive responses teach others what works best (for example, "I need to see your face" or "Please say that again"). These requests can be phrased gently, with words like *please* or *it would be helpful*, or stated more directly, depending on the person's style and comfort level.

Apologetic responses ("Sorry, I didn't hear you") unintentionally teach that the breakdown was their fault.

Frustrated responses teach others to avoid conversations altogether.

Clear, direct responses show others exactly how to communicate in ways that work.

Even if unhelpful patterns have developed in long-standing relationships, every new interaction is a fresh opportunity to reset. With each conversation, your communication partner is teaching others how to treat them.

Why Communication with Hearing Loss is Different

Communicating with someone who has hearing loss isn't intuitive. What works for one person doesn't always work for another. People assume the strategies they use with their grandmother, or with someone else they know with hearing loss, will work the same here. That's not necessarily the case.

Add to this the fact that in hearing culture, communication is expected to be quick, invisible, and effortless, and many assume hearing aids or cochlear implants "fix" hearing loss. These assumptions put pressure on people with hearing loss to apologize or cover up. In reality, for people with hearing loss, communication is not automatic. Communication with hearing loss requires intentional adjustments from everyone involved. I encourage you to see the blessing in this. In a world where our attentions are infinitely divided and distracted as we multitask, slowing down in mindful communication with another person creates a more effective and meaningful connection.

Communication Strategies & Communication Repair

In addition to hearing aids, cochlear implants, assistive listening devices, accommodations, or other technology, there are simple but impactful communication strategies that make conversation easier. You are probably aware of many and know they significantly help your friend hear and understand. The challenge for them is often asking for what they need. This is called self-advocacy, which is defined by the National Deaf Center as "the ability to articulate one's needs and make informed decisions about the support necessary to meet those needs."

It is far more effective for your friend to tell people what they need (for example, "please speak clearly," or "I need to see your face,") than to tell them what's wrong (such as "I can't hear you," or "you're mumbling") or what not to do (like "don't whisper," or "don't shout"). The more specific and efficient their suggestions, the easier it will be for others to respond helpfully.

Encourage and model this by responding positively when they make requests or by rephrasing unclear communication yourself. Notice when a situation calls for clarification and support them in speaking up.

The goal is to have quick, clear, and easy phrases ready to use. Polite lead-ins like *"please," "would you kindly,"* or *"it would help me if…"* make requests sound natural and respectful, if this is important. Here are a few highly effective suggestions.

Common Effective Communication Requests

"Speak clearly."

"You need my full attention before you start talking."

"I need to see your face."

"Please talk to me only when we're in the same room."

"Speak louder."

"Speak without gum or food in your mouth."

"Trim your mustache/beard so I can see your lips."

"Turn down the TV/radio/music."

Common Communication Repair Requests

"Can you repeat what you said?"

"Could you rephrase that?"

"Could you simplify what you just said?"

"I heard x, y, and z, but I missed ____."

- **When they ask you to repeat something**, don't sigh, roll your eyes, or say "never mind." Make this your default, every time.

- **When they successfully advocate for themselves**, asking a server to turn down music, requesting captions at a meeting, explaining what they need, don't jump in to "help." Afterward, acknowledge it: "That was clear. I could tell they understood."

- **When communication breaks down in front of others**, stay calm. Your reaction sets the tone. If you stay patient, others will follow. If you show frustration, they'll assume frustration is acceptable.

- **If someone else responds poorly**, sighing, dismissing, or saying "never mind", gently model the alternative: "Let me try saying that differently" or "Here, I'll repeat it."

ALLY INSIGHTS

- When my loved one asks me to repeat myself, what is my first internal reaction—before I respond out loud? Patience? Annoyance? Resignation?

- Have I ever felt like communication breakdowns are their problem to solve? What would change if I truly believed it was a shared responsibility?

In *Becoming Hearing Empowered*, your loved one completes three activities under **Teaching People How to Treat Me: Asking for Accommodations**, **Teaching Communication Strategies**, and **Practicing Communication Repair**. They develop specific phrases to use in different situations.

If they're open to practicing together, ask: "Would you like to try some of these phrases with me so they feel more natural?"

Role-playing can feel awkward at first, but it helps the words become automatic. Try a few scenarios: a noisy restaurant, a work meeting, a family gathering. Let them lead, and you play the other person. Afterward, ask what felt easy and what still feels clunky. This isn't about getting it perfect; it's about building confidence through repetition.

If they'd rather not role-play, simply ask: "Which communication strategies matter most to you, and how do I reinforce them when we're together?"

Section 4: "Selective Hearing"

ALLY PERSPECTIVE: WHY THIS MATTERS

People with hearing loss are often accused of having "selective hearing" or only hearing when they "want to." For someone with hearing loss, this accusation feels deeply hurtful. It suggests that their ability to understand depends on motivation or effort, rather than the real challenges of hearing loss and communication. Understanding what's really happening equips you to counter these misconceptions and to support your loved one with patience and respect.

When a parent asks a child with hearing loss to clean their room and the child doesn't respond, but that same child easily understands when told it's time for dinner, there are many factors at play. The brain relies on countless external cues to fill in missed auditory information, so context and timing make a big difference. For most messages, the cognitive effort required to understand spoken language is significantly higher than for a person with typical hearing.

If your friend with hearing loss is working at their desk around 5:30 p.m. and smells dinner cooking, then hears "-ime –er," the brain logically fills in the blanks: "Time for dinner!" But if it's 9:30 a.m. on a Saturday and they hear "--oom!" without any context, it could mean, "I'm on a Zoom call," "Where's the broom?" or "Clean the bathroom."

Additionally, if your friend is not focusing their attention on what is said, the words don't have meaning and sound like gibberish.

Focusing attention on spoken language is called **auditory attention**, and it requires active mental engagement in a way many hearing people don't realize. Your friend has learned how to do this naturally, often without even thinking about it, but after sustained listening in challenging environments, they feel exhausted. This is called **listening fatigue**, and it's a very real experience. It will be discussed further in Chapter Eight, but for now, it's important for you to understand what it is and to help others understand it, too.

"Selective hearing" is better explained as **selective auditory attention**. The difference matters: "selective hearing" implies your friend *chooses* to hear only what interests them. Selective auditory attention describes something very different: without focused attention *before* speech begins, the brain doesn't process sounds into meaningful language. It's not that your friend heard you and decided to ignore it; it's that the words never registered as language in the first place. The times your friend has been accused of not listening were probably times when the speaker failed to get their full attention before talking. Encouraging and supporting your friend, as they ask people to attain their full attention before they speak, helps teach others how to communicate with respect and appreciation for their hearing needs—and for the extra effort it takes to understand.

- **Reject the myth:** Never accuse or joke about "selective hearing." It dismisses the real effort your loved one is making.

- **Explain to others:** If family, friends, or coworkers make this accusation, calmly explain that it's actually about context and auditory attention.

- **Secure attention first:** Model good habits by making sure your loved one is focused before you start speaking.

ALLY INSIGHTS

- Have I ever teased my communication partner about "selective hearing"? How might that have felt to them?

- Do I fully understand how exhausting auditory attention and listening fatigue are?

- How do I model better communication habits so others learn from me?

In the *Becoming Hearing Empowered* journal activity **"Selective Hearing" Reflection**, your friend with hearing loss reflects on these questions:

- How did it feel to learn about "selective hearing," listening fatigue, and auditory attention?

- Are there people in your life who need to hear this message?

- How will you communicate it to them?

Join the conversation by asking:

- "How do you feel when people accuse you of selective hearing?"

- "Do you want to practice together how we explain this clearly when it comes up?"

By standing beside them in these moments, you show that you see their effort, respect their experience, and won't let harmful misconceptions go unchallenged.

Section 5: Places

Every environment shapes how your loved one hears, but those same barriers often go unnoticed by people without hearing loss. When you learn to spot noise, lighting, and seating challenges, you not only help improve access in the moment, you also show your loved one that their experience is valid and worth planning around. Your awareness makes daily life less stressful and more enjoyable for both of you.

Every new location your loved one enters is its own unique listening environment. Many factors affect how well, or how little, they can hear and understand in that space. Considering these factors and analyzing the physical environment ahead of time allows them (and you) to make a plan to ensure they have the best access possible.

Analyzing a listening environment means paying attention to several key factors. **Lighting** affects lipreading; dim restaurants or backlit speakers make visual cues harder to catch. **Background noise** includes obvious sources like music and crowds, but also HVAC systems, kitchen clatter, and traffic from nearby windows. **Acoustics** matter too: hard surfaces like tile, glass, and concrete create echo and reverberation that muddy speech, while carpeting, curtains, and soft furnishings absorb echoes. **Layout** determines sight lines—can your loved one see the speaker's face, or are there obstructions? **Distance** from the speaker affects how well sound reaches them, and **seating position** influences everything: proximity to noise sources, access to the better-hearing ear, and ability to see everyone in a group.

A frustrating setting is often improved by taking a few minutes to identify the sources of difficulty and thinking about what changes to make in the future. For particularly challenging environments, hearing aids and cochlear implants actually make listening more difficult. Background noise is amplified along with speech because the devices can't distinguish which sounds to focus on. Bringing this information to an audiologist can prompt programming changes to their devices, or a suggestion for an accessory. In some cases, after weighing all the options, your loved one may decide that a certain location simply isn't enjoyable or worth the struggle—and that's a valid choice too.

In the following pages, you'll find an entire section titled **"My Places."** It includes multiple copies of a worksheet that guides you (and your loved one) in analyzing specific places and determining listening needs in each. A table of contents is available on the first page so you can jot down the names of the places you've analyzed, along with a list of suggested locations.

You can complete these worksheets on your own to build awareness of how environments affect communication, or work through them alongside your loved one to compare notes. For now, choose one location to analyze and complete, then continue the section on the page immediately following the My Places worksheets. An example of this journal activity is found at the end of this section.

MY PLACES

MY PLACES - TABLE OF CONTENTS

	Description of Place
1	
2	
3	
4	
5	
6	
7	
8	
9	
10	

MY PLACES - PLACE SUGGESTIONS

- in a therapist's office
- a bar
- in the car
- in the kitchen
- in the bedroom
- when watching TV
- outside
- at work
- online
- in a small store
- in the grocery store
- in a large box store
- at the shopping mall
- in a restaurant
- on a walk
- walking with more than one person
- at the gym
- in the classroom (as a student)
- in a doctor's office
- as a presenter/speaker/teacher
- at the beach
- at the pool
- when camping
- around the fire pit
- on the bus
- at the airport
- on a boat
- on a train
- when gardening
- attending a sports event
- at the movie theater
- on a run
- on a bike ride
- at a hotel

Place: ____

Map out main features of the location. Mark sources of interfering noise with an "X" or star.

Lighting: bright, normal, dim, dark, flashing, backlighting, ____

Acoustics: clear, echo-y, windy, sudden bursts, ____

Number of People: me, 2, small group 3-5, medium group 6-10, large group 11-20, crowd 20+ _______________

Background Noise: silent, murmur, chatter, commotion, ruckus, roar, ________________________________

Main Players:

_________________ Speech: high, low, quiet, loud, mumbles, fast, facial hair, _______________

_________________ Speech: high, low, quiet, loud, mumbles, fast, facial hair, _______________

_________________ Speech: high, low, quiet, loud, mumbles, fast, facial hair, _______________

_________________ Speech: high, low, quiet, loud, mumbles, fast, facial hair, _______________

_________________ Speech: high, low, quiet, loud, mumbles, fast, facial hair, _______________

Communication Mode: entertainment, instructional, informational, intimate, conversational, practical, other:

____

What main factors make this space challenging for you to hear, understand, and feel included?

Use a highlighter or pen to circle them.

What changes could be made that would help you enjoy the activity and space?

____

____

Is there assistive listening technology or accommodations that could be helpful?
Remote mic, new program on hearing aid/cochlear implant processor, auto-caption app on my phone, real time
captioning service, change seating, other:

____

____

What could my main player(s) do to help me hear, understand and feel included?

____

____

Are there safety concerns? hearing protection, visual alerts for emergency situations, medic alert to inform
emergency workers of your needs, other:

____

____

Action plan:

____

____

____

Let it go?

____

____

Place: ____

Map out main features of the location. Mark sources of interfering noise with an "X" or star.

Lighting: bright, normal, dim, dark, flashing, backlighting, ____

Acoustics: clear, echo-y, windy, sudden bursts, ____

Number of People: me, 2, small group 3-5, medium group 6-10, large group 11-20, crowd 20+ ________________

Background Noise: silent, murmur, chatter, commotion, ruckus, roar, ___________________________________

Main Players:

_________________ Speech: high, low, quiet, loud, mumbles, fast, facial hair, _________________

_________________ Speech: high, low, quiet, loud, mumbles, fast, facial hair, _________________

_________________ Speech: high, low, quiet, loud, mumbles, fast, facial hair, _________________

_________________ Speech: high, low, quiet, loud, mumbles, fast, facial hair, _________________

_________________ Speech: high, low, quiet, loud, mumbles, fast, facial hair, _________________

Communication Mode: entertainment, instructional, informational, intimate, conversational, practical, other:

____

What main factors make this space challenging for you to hear, understand, and feel included?

Use a highlighter or pen to circle them.

What changes could be made that would help you enjoy the activity and space?

____

____

Is there assistive listening technology or accommodations that could be helpful?
Remote mic, new program on hearing aid/cochlear implant processor, auto-caption app on my phone, real time captioning service, change seating, other:

____

____

What could my main player(s) do to help me hear, understand and feel included?

____

____

Are there safety concerns? hearing protection, visual alerts for emergency situations, medic alert to inform emergency workers of your needs, other:

____

____

Action plan:

____

____

____

Let it go?

____

____

Place: ____

Map out main features of the location. Mark sources of interfering noise with an "X" or star.

Lighting: bright, normal, dim, dark, flashing, backlighting, ____

Acoustics: clear, echo-y, windy, sudden bursts, ____

Number of People: me, 2, small group 3-5, medium group 6-10, large group 11-20, crowd 20+ _______________

Background Noise: silent, murmur, chatter, commotion, ruckus, roar, ________________________________

Main Players:

___________________ Speech: high, low, quiet, loud, mumbles, fast, facial hair, ___________________

___________________ Speech: high, low, quiet, loud, mumbles, fast, facial hair, ___________________

___________________ Speech: high, low, quiet, loud, mumbles, fast, facial hair, ___________________

___________________ Speech: high, low, quiet, loud, mumbles, fast, facial hair, ___________________

___________________ Speech: high, low, quiet, loud, mumbles, fast, facial hair, ___________________

Communication Mode: entertainment, instructional, informational, intimate, conversational, practical, other:

____

What main factors make this space challenging for you to hear, understand, and feel included?

Use a highlighter or pen to circle them.

What changes could be made that would help you enjoy the activity and space?

____

____

Is there assistive listening technology or accommodations that could be helpful?
Remote mic, new program on hearing aid/cochlear implant processor, auto-caption app on my phone, real time captioning service, change seating, other:

____

____

What could my main player(s) do to help me hear, understand and feel included?

____

____

Are there safety concerns? hearing protection, visual alerts for emergency situations, medic alert to inform emergency workers of your needs, other:

____

____

Action plan:

____

____

____

Let it go?

____

____

Place: ____

Map out main features of the location. Mark sources of interfering noise with an "X" or star.

Lighting: bright, normal, dim, dark, flashing, backlighting, ___________________________________

Acoustics: clear, echo-y, windy, sudden bursts, ____

Number of People: me, 2, small group 3-5, medium group 6-10, large group 11-20, crowd 20+ ______________

Background Noise: silent, murmur, chatter, commotion, ruckus, roar, ______________________________

Main Players:

_____________________ Speech: high, low, quiet, loud, mumbles, fast, facial hair, _____________________

_____________________ Speech: high, low, quiet, loud, mumbles, fast, facial hair, _____________________

_____________________ Speech: high, low, quiet, loud, mumbles, fast, facial hair, _____________________

_____________________ Speech: high, low, quiet, loud, mumbles, fast, facial hair, _____________________

_____________________ Speech: high, low, quiet, loud, mumbles, fast, facial hair, _____________________

Communication Mode: entertainment, instructional, informational, intimate, conversational, practical, other:

____

What main factors make this space challenging for you to hear, understand, and feel included?

Use a highlighter or pen to circle them.

What changes could be made that would help you enjoy the activity and space?

____

____

Is there assistive listening technology or accommodations that could be helpful?
Remote mic, new program on hearing aid/cochlear implant processor, auto-caption app on my phone, real time captioning service, change seating, other:

____

____

What could my main player(s) do to help me hear, understand and feel included?

____

____

Are there safety concerns? hearing protection, visual alerts for emergency situations, medic alert to inform emergency workers of your needs, other:

____

____

Action plan:

____

____

____

Let it go?

____

____

Place: ____

Map out main features of the location. Mark sources of interfering noise with an "X" or star.

Lighting: bright, normal, dim, dark, flashing, backlighting, ____

Acoustics: clear, echo-y, windy, sudden bursts, ____

Number of People: me, 2, small group 3-5, medium group 6-10, large group 11-20, crowd 20+ ________________

Background Noise: silent, murmur, chatter, commotion, ruckus, roar, ____________________________________

Main Players:

____________________ Speech: high, low, quiet, loud, mumbles, fast, facial hair, ____________________

____________________ Speech: high, low, quiet, loud, mumbles, fast, facial hair, ____________________

____________________ Speech: high, low, quiet, loud, mumbles, fast, facial hair, ____________________

____________________ Speech: high, low, quiet, loud, mumbles, fast, facial hair, ____________________

____________________ Speech: high, low, quiet, loud, mumbles, fast, facial hair, ____________________

Communication Mode: entertainment, instructional, informational, intimate, conversational, practical, other:

____

What main factors make this space challenging for you to hear, understand, and feel included?

Use a highlighter or pen to circle them.

What changes could be made that would help you enjoy the activity and space?

____

____

Is there assistive listening technology or accommodations that could be helpful?
Remote mic, new program on hearing aid/cochlear implant processor, auto-caption app on my phone, real time
captioning service, change seating, other:

____

____

What could my main player(s) do to help me hear, understand and feel included?

____

____

Are there safety concerns? hearing protection, visual alerts for emergency situations, medic alert to inform
emergency workers of your needs, other:

____

____

Action plan:

____

____

____

Let it go?

____

____

- **Support planning:** Help brainstorm accommodations or adjustments before visiting a challenging place.

- **Advocate with respect:** If your friend wants support, ask staff about captioning devices, loop systems, or quieter seating.

- **Validate tough choices:** Back them up if they decide a certain place just isn't enjoyable or worth the effort.

ALLY INSIGHTS

- How aware am I of the listening challenges in different places we go together?

- Have I unintentionally overlooked barriers because they don't affect me directly?

- Do I support my friend's decisions when they choose to leave early, take breaks, or avoid certain places?

Ask your friend about the places they are reflecting on in their **My Places** worksheets.

- Which environments feel comfortable and supportive?

- Which ones are stressful or difficult?

- What makes the difference?

Listening to their insights helps you understand how much lighting, background noise, and layout affect communication.

Use what you learn to be more aware of access in your shared spaces. When you notice barriers or see opportunities for improvement, support their choices and help create environments that feel easier and more inclusive.

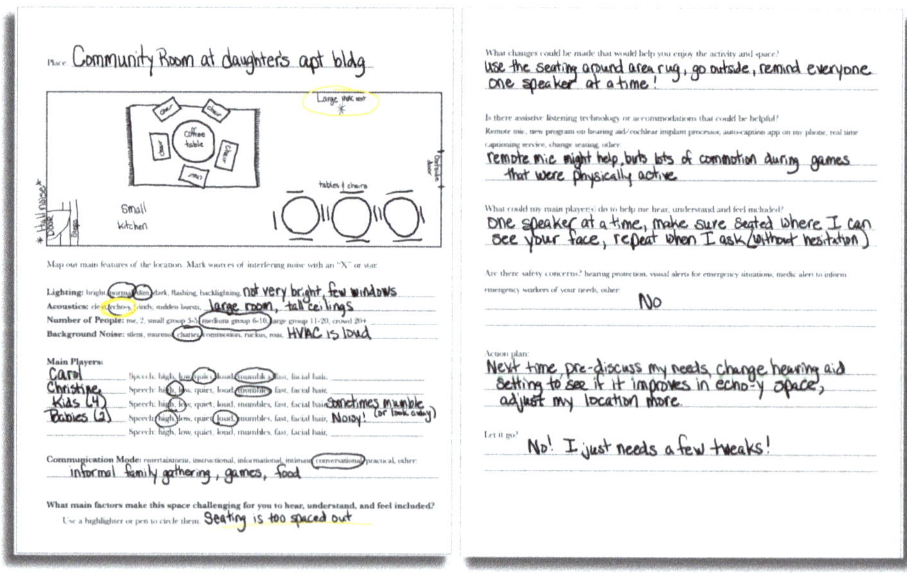

A Word About Rights

Know that your loved one has specific legal rights as a person with a hearing disability. These protections ensure they cannot be excluded or discriminated against because of their hearing loss, and they guarantee access to accommodations in many settings.

Section 504 of the Rehabilitation Act of 1973

This is a federal civil rights law that prevents discrimination against people with disabilities in federally funded jobs, programs, and activities. It covers almost all universities, colleges, and career training programs (because most receive taxpayer funding). It also applies to many employers, such as hospitals, nursing homes, and public schools, that receive federal assistance. In practice, this means your loved one cannot be turned away from a program or job if they otherwise qualify, and they are entitled to accommodations such as captioning, notetakers, interpreters, and assistive listening devices when needed for equal access.

The Americans with Disabilities Act (ADA), 1990

This law prohibits discrimination against people with disabilities in employment, transportation, public accommodations, communications, and access to state and local government programs. It protects the right to reasonable accommodations in most public spaces.

If rights are violated:

If your loved one's rights to access are denied, they do not have to simply accept it. They can request clarification, file complaints, or seek advocacy help. Support them by researching options, accompanying them in difficult conversations, or helping them find advocacy resources.

Check out **hearingoutloud.net/resources** for helpful resource links.

- **Learn the basics:** Familiarize yourself with Section 504 and the ADA so you can help reinforce your friend's rights.

- **Back them up:** If someone pushes back on providing accommodations, be prepared to calmly remind them that access is a legal requirement.

- **Research resources:** Help identify local or national advocacy organizations that provide support.

- **Encourage empowerment:** Remind your friend that asking for accommodations isn't asking for favors, it's exercising their rights.

- Do I fully understand that accommodations are rights, not optional extras?

- How comfortable am I helping my friend assert those rights in real-world situations?

- If access is denied, how do I best support? Through quiet encouragement, helping with research, standing beside my loved one in advocacy, or guiding them toward legal or professional advocacy resources that help protect their rights?

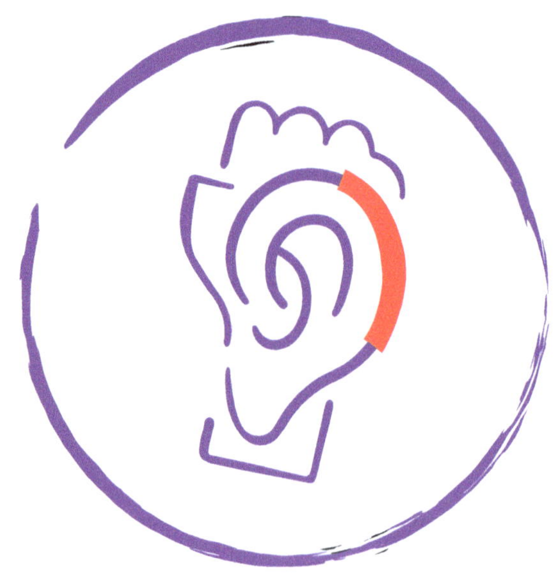

8 | self-care

The kids' birthday party had been a success. My son played with his friends, opened presents, blew out candles. He seemed happy.

But an hour after everyone left, I found him in his room with the lights off, still in his party clothes, staring at the ceiling.

"You okay?" I asked.

He nodded. "Just need quiet."

He was eleven. He'd spent three hours straining to hear his friends over music and screaming and overlapping voices.

He'd smiled through all of it. And now he had nothing left.

I sat on the edge of his bed and didn't say anything. I didn't need to. I just stayed there, letting the silence be enough.

Section 1: Listening Fatigue

ALLY PERSPECTIVE: WHY THIS MATTERS

Listening fatigue isn't about attitude, it's about brainwork. When you recognize that exhaustion comes from constant effort to understand speech and not from lack of interest, you respond with empathy instead of frustration. Supporting breaks and recharging activities helps your loved one preserve energy for connection, not just survival.

Self-care is the intentional practice of protecting and improving one's own well-being, both physically and emotionally. For your loved one, self-care goes beyond general wellness habits. It involves strategies tailored to the unique challenges of living with hearing loss.

Hearing loss significantly impacts communication and relationships, even in the closest circles. Misunderstandings and missed exchanges create strain, not because of lack of effort, but because their energy is taxed in ways most hearing people never experience.

That's why self-care matters. It provides your loved one with a toolbox of strategies to replenish themselves after the draining effects of fatigue and social effort. This chapter will help you understand key areas of self-care specific to living with hearing loss and show you how to support your loved one in practicing them.

Hearing loss, of any degree, creates an excessive drain on energy when your loved one is communicating in spoken (rather than signed) language. You notice that after a social gathering, a family event, or a full day at work, they seem mentally exhausted and crave quiet time or solitary activities. This exhaustion isn't laziness or moodiness. It's called listening fatigue, and it's very real.

Listening fatigue occurs because the brain has to work harder to make sense of incomplete or distorted auditory signals. When background noise is present, this effect is even stronger. Research shows that while the primary auditory cortex (the part of the brain that processes sound) is under-activated in people with hearing loss, the prefrontal cortex (responsible for language comprehension) works overtime.

That means your loved one's brain is constantly filling in missing pieces using context clues, facial expressions, mouth shapes, and other non-verbal cues. While this compensation allows them to follow conversations, it comes at a cost:

- Reduced auditory memory (remembering what was said)

- Reduced working memory (holding short-term information to perform a task, like writing down numbers)

- Reduced ability to sustain attention and fully comprehend speech

The result? Their brain ends up exhausted just from the effort of trying to communicate.

Combating Listening Fatigue

One of the most effective strategies is to schedule listening breaks: activities that don't require them to decode speech or respond verbally. These breaks are short (five minutes) or longer (an hour), depending on the situation and the level of fatigue.

Common activities that help recharge include:

- Taking a walk (with or without music, audiobooks, or podcasts)

- Arts and crafts (painting, sewing, knitting, etc.)

- Watching TV with captions

- Adult coloring books or journaling

- Meditation or mindfulness exercises

- Video games

- Taking a nap

It's important to note: these activities should be used intentionally for rest and recovery, not as a way to withdraw from life altogether. You can help by encouraging balance, supporting breaks when needed, and respecting the purpose behind them.

ALLY IN ACTION

- **After a long day**, a social event, or a challenging meeting, don't ask "What's wrong?" or "Why are you so quiet?" Instead, try: "You've been listening hard all day. Do you want some quiet time, or would company help?"

- **Protect transition time.** When they get home from work or a draining outing, give them 15-20 minutes before starting a conversation that requires focus. Let them decompress first.

- **Suggest breaks before they're desperate.** At family gatherings or parties, check in: "Want to step outside for a few minutes?" Don't wait until they've hit a wall.

- **When you notice them zoning out or giving short answers**, resist the urge to take it personally. Say nothing, or simply: "I see you're running low. We don't have to talk right now."

- Think of a time I felt annoyed that they seemed "checked out" or uninterested. Looking back, what had their day looked like? What did I miss?

- Do I treat their need for quiet time as rejection, or as a reasonable response to invisible effort?

In *Becoming Hearing Empowered*, your loved one completes the activity **Combating Listening Fatigue**. They identify times of day when a listening break would help, brainstorm restorative activities, and create an action plan.

If they're open to sharing, ask: "What does it feel like when listening fatigue hits, and what helps you recover?"

This question invites them to describe their experience in their own words, rather than simply naming a time or activity. Listen for cues about what recharges them: walks, silence, TV with captions, creative projects, and look for ways to build those into your shared routine. Also share what you've observed: "I've noticed you seem most drained after ____. Is that accurate?"

Their fatigue isn't about you. Understanding that, truly believing it, is one of the most important shifts you can make.

Section 2: Self-Disclosure Fatigue

Talking about hearing loss takes effort, especially when your friend has to explain it to others again and again. Each disclosure is a small act of trust, and the reactions they receive make it easier, or harder, to keep sharing. When you remember what they've told you, and support them in those conversations with others, you help make communication smoother and less tiring for everyone involved.

Self-disclosure, the act of telling others about hearing loss, is a vital strategy for your friend to get the accommodations they need. But it comes with a cost. Repeatedly having to explain their hearing loss, especially to new people or to people who continually forget, causes stress, anxiety, and fatigue.

Your friend may struggle with 'what if' worries before self-disclosing: *What if they get annoyed? What if they tease me or gossip about me? What if it doesn't make a difference? What if they think less of me?* This anxiety makes them avoid disclosure altogether, or resort to bluffing (pretending to understand).

Even when disclosure does happen, the responses they get can add to the fatigue:

- **Excessive sympathy:** "Oh, that must be so sad."

- **Dismissal or disbelief:** "You don't look like you have hearing loss."

- **Testing behavior:** Insisting your friend "proves" they have hearing loss by covering their mouth to see if they can lipread.

- **Tangents:** Stories about someone else's hearing loss or having an experience with temporary hearing loss with a head cold, derailing the conversation.

Add to this the frustration of having to remind the same people again and again, even those who care deeply about them, and it's easy to see how draining this becomes. While loved ones vow to do better, old habits are hard to break, especially in the excitement of conversations or noisy gatherings.

Combating Self-Disclosure Fatigue

Practice makes disclosure easier. Planning what to say in advance, and even rehearsing it (as covered in Chapter 7), helps build confidence. Nonverbal strategies, like pins, decorated hearing devices, or T-shirts, also ease the load.

For people who frequently forget, it helps to have a calm, intentional conversation. The goal is mutual understanding, not blame. Sharing feelings ("I feel left out when you forget to slow down") is more effective than pointing fingers.

Some people agree on simple reminder cues, like a shoulder tap or ear gesture, to quickly trigger the memory that communication strategies are needed. This saves energy and reduces tension.

- **Acknowledge the effort:** Understand that disclosure takes courage and energy.

- **Listen without derailing:** Don't shift the focus to yourself, someone you know, or unrelated stories. Stay with their experience.

- **Respect nonverbal cues:** If your friend uses a signal with you, respond quickly without frustration.

- **Help break habits:** If you're someone who forgets, commit to improvement, and accept reminders gracefully.

ALLY INSIGHTS

- How do I usually respond when my friend explains their hearing loss to others?

- What do I do to make those moments of disclosure less stressful or repetitive for them?

- How do I support my friend when others forget, react poorly, or change the subject?

In *Becoming Hearing Empowered,* your friend's journal activity **Combating Self-Disclosure Fatigue** asks them to:

- Reflect on how self-disclosure fatigue has affected their life.

- Consider whether there are conversations they could have with people who made disclosure difficult.

Ask:

- "Would you like to share what you wrote about self-disclosure fatigue?"

- "How do I make disclosure easier for you when we're together?"

- "Would a simple reminder cue help us in situations where I might forget?"

Even if they don't want to share their writing, just asking shows you respect their effort and are committed to supporting them.

Section 3: Self-Advocacy Fatigue

Speaking up for access takes courage, persistence, and energy. Your communication partner advocates repeatedly for things most people take for granted, and that constant effort wears them down. When you recognize how draining self-advocacy is and share some of the responsibility, by listening, supporting, or reinforcing their requests, you help make inclusion feel like a team effort instead of a solo task.

Self-advocacy often comes right after self-disclosure. Once your communication partner tells someone about their hearing loss, they usually have to explain what communication strategies work best or request specific accommodations.

This is an incredibly important skill, but it's also exhausting. Self-advocacy is difficult for many reasons. If the other person is in a position of authority (a boss, professor, or supervisor), your communication partner may feel intimidated. If they make a request and it isn't honored, they feel anger, frustration, and the added burden of problem-solving on the spot. If they are naturally shy or introverted, speaking up feels overwhelming. And they may hesitate to speak up because they don't want to hurt someone's feelings when asking for a change.

The reality is, for someone with hearing loss, self-advocacy is rarely optional. Without it, they risk feeling isolated, ignored, and forgotten. But having to continually speak up, explain, and insist, day after day, creates its own kind of fatigue.

It's also frustrating because it never ends. Even when a request is honored one time, it isn't the next:

- A saved front-row seat for lipreading is given away because they arrived five minutes late.

- A captioned film is forgotten in class, and apologies roll in while the access they needed is missing.

Each time, they are faced with deciding whether to speak up again, or let it go at the cost of frustration and exclusion.

The old adage "the squeaky wheel gets the grease" is especially true here. The more your communication partner advocates, the more likely people are to make accessibility part of their routine. But the flip side is also true: despite their requests and even the protection of laws, accommodations are refused. Discrimination happens.

When it does, they are not alone. Agencies, advocacy groups, and legal professionals are available to step in to help enforce rights. But engaging in this kind of advocacy, on top of everyday self-advocacy, is both exhausting and, at times, empowering.

Check out **hearingoutloud.net/resources** for helpful resource links.

Combating Self-Advocacy Fatigue

Regardless of how often your communication partner has to do it, self-advocacy is exhausting, and it's important to recognize and validate their feelings about it. Just as with self-disclosure, practice does make advocating easier and easier. Perhaps sending email requests versus talking directly to a person is the best way for them. Enlisting the help of a friend, an advisor, or a coworker can make the job a little less daunting. They may need the help of a professional disability advocate or lawyer.

Knowing they need to ask for help in the form of accommodations feels less "needy" if it's balanced with opportunities to give help and support to others. Keep in mind that even though self-advocacy feels uncomfortable, both asking for and offering help is a pillar of self-care and a cornerstone to building community.

- **Before an event or appointment where advocacy is needed**, ask: "Do you want me to handle the accommodation request this time, or would you rather do it yourself?" Let them choose, don't assume.

- **When you see an opportunity to advocate**, take it without being asked. Turn on captions when you start the movie. Request a quieter table when you check in at the restaurant. These small acts lift weight they don't even realize they're carrying.

- **When they've just finished advocating**, whether it went well or not, acknowledge the effort, not just the outcome. "That took energy. How are you feeling?"

- **When they're too tired to push back**, don't say "You should have said something." Just be present. Later, ask: "Would it help if I spoke up in situations like that?"

ALLY INSIGHTS

- When I notice an opportunity to advocate for my loved one, what holds me back—not wanting to overstep, not thinking of it, or something else?

- Do I view their need for advocacy as a burden I help carry, or as their problem that I occasionally assist with? What's the difference?

In *Becoming Hearing Empowered*, your loved one completes the activity **Combating Self-Advocacy Fatigue**. They reflect on their feelings about self-advocacy, including resentment, exhaustion, but also the confidence it builds.

If they're open to sharing, ask: "When it comes to advocating for your hearing needs, what do you wish you didn't have to do alone?"

This question gives them permission to name the parts that feel heaviest, without assuming you know what those are. Their answer might surprise you. It's often not the big asks (requesting interpreters, filing complaints) but the small, constant ones (reminding the same coworker for the tenth time, always being the one to ask for captions).

Whatever they share, resist the urge to promise you'll fix it. Instead, ask: "How would it feel if I handled that one for a while?" Then follow through.

Section 4: Technology Fatigue

ALLY PERSPECTIVE: WHY THIS MATTERS

Technology makes hearing possible in remarkable ways, but it also adds new layers of stress. Learning, maintaining, and troubleshooting hearing devices is mentally and physically tiring for your loved one. When you understand this hidden effort and offer steady, practical support, you help turn technology from a source of frustration into a tool for connection and confidence.

In today's rapidly advancing technological world, devices meant to enhance our quality of life are constantly evolving. For hearing aid and cochlear implant users, these improvements bring better sound quality, comfort, and connectivity. But with these benefits comes an often-overlooked downside: technology fatigue. This is the physical and mental exhaustion that comes from managing complex, ever-changing technology.

Modern hearing aids and CIs include Bluetooth, smartphone apps, noise-canceling algorithms, and even artificial intelligence that adapts automatically to environments. While these features improve listening, they can be overwhelming, especially for those less familiar with modern tech. Learning to navigate settings, connect devices, and troubleshoot issues takes time, focus, and patience. Even small tasks, like adjusting volumes or pairing to a phone, feel demanding, especially when they happen mid-conversation or in busy settings.

Physical fatigue also sets in. Continuous device use causes ear discomfort, headaches, or soreness. Maintenance adds more work: cleaning, charging, updating, or repairing devices becomes stressful, particularly for those with dexterity or vision challenges. When repairs are needed, long waits for appointments or shipping delays leave your loved one without access altogether.

The psychological toll is real. Frustration, dependence, or feelings of inadequacy surface when technology fails. Some people even stop using their devices, losing out on the benefits they provide. Rapid updates and upgrades add pressure and make devices feel outdated too quickly, creating financial and emotional strain.

Combating Technology Fatigue

Technology fatigue can significantly affect your loved one's confidence and comfort, but there are ways to help.

Many manufacturers now emphasize user-friendly design and clear instructions. If your loved one is exploring new devices, encourage them to ask their audiologist about brands with strong customer support. Personalized training and follow-up appointments also make a big difference, though these take persistence to arrange.

Encourage your loved one to connect with local or online support groups, such as the Hearing Loss Association of America (HLAA), or find a hearing loss buddy for practical, peer-based help. Also assist by learning about the technology yourself or helping them connect with a tech-savvy friend or family member. Collaboration builds confidence, and connection.

Online videos and user communities also ease frustration. Searching YouTube or joining social media groups for specific device brands often yields quick, helpful solutions.

Finally, remember that technology fatigue isn't just technical, it's emotional. If your loved one feels overwhelmed, encouraging them to step away for a bit helps them return to their devices with a clearer mind and renewed patience.

ALLY IN ACTION

- **Be a tech partner:** Offer to sit down and learn the device functions alongside your loved one.

- **Help troubleshoot:** Look up instructions, watch YouTube tutorials together, or search forums when issues arise.

- **Be patient:** Understand that frustration with devices is not just "user error." It's a real form of fatigue.

- **Assist with maintenance:** Offer to help with cleaning, charging routines, or even scheduling repair appointments.

- Do I underestimate how draining it is for my loved one to manage their devices?

- Have I ever shown frustration when they struggled with tech, instead of offering patience?

- How comfortable am I helping them troubleshoot or learn something new?

In *Becoming Hearing Empowered,* your loved one's journal activity **Combating Technology Fatigue** asks them to reflect on:

- Whether technology fatigue is something they've experienced.

- How it has caused stress in their life.

- Which strategies from this section might help.

Ask:

- "What parts of using your devices feel most stressful?"

- "Would you like me to learn the basics too, so I can help when needed?"

- "Should we make a plan for maintenance or repairs together so it doesn't fall all on you?"

Section 5: The Cost of Bluffing & Creating Boundaries

Bluffing and boundary-setting seem like opposites—one hides limits, the other declares them—but both are ways your friend with hearing loss manages energy and belonging. Bluffing often protects against embarrassment or awkwardness, while boundaries protect well-being. Make honesty feel safe and boundaries feel respected by checking in, supporting their need for breaks or quieter settings, and showing that saying "I didn't catch that" or "I need to skip this event" keeps connection real, not difficult.

The Cost of Bluffing

Bluffing is when someone with hearing loss pretends to understand by nodding, smiling, or laughing along, even when they didn't catch what was said. The word "bluff" is defined as "trying to deceive someone as to one's abilities or intentions." It's a survival strategy most people with hearing loss have used at some point, but it comes at a cost.

When your friend bluffs, it sends the message: *"I heard and understood you."* Over time, this creates the illusion that their hearing is better than it really is. If others believe they always understand, it becomes harder to secure needed accommodations or modifications in communication. Bluffing also backfires, like when they can't answer a question about the very topic they just pretended to follow.

For you, it's important to understand why bluffing happens:

- To avoid embarrassment or stigma.

- To escape the effort of constant self-disclosure.

- To prevent awkwardness or frustration for others.

But while bluffing feels easier in the moment, it often leaves your friend excluded and misunderstood.

- **Notice the signs:** If your friend nods silently without engaging, check in: "Do you want me to repeat or summarize?"

- **Normalize clarification:** Show that asking for repeats is no big deal by modeling it yourself.

- **Don't tease:** Avoid jokes about bluffing. It adds shame and makes disclosure harder.

- Do I let bluffing slide because it feels easier for me too?

- How do I make it safer for my friend to admit when they didn't catch something?

- Have I ever teased them for bluffing? How do I repair that?

In *Becoming Hearing Empowered*, your friend's journal activity **Bluffing** asks them to reflect on:

- When and why they bluff.

- What they are missing because of it.

- How replacing bluffing with self-disclosure or self-advocacy could change their relationships.

Ask:

- "Do you want to share times when you feel you bluff the most?"

- "How do I help make those situations easier?"

Creating Boundaries

Living with hearing loss is tiring, not just because of listening effort, but also repeated self-disclosure and self-advocacy. That's why boundaries are essential.

A boundary is like an invisible line protecting your communication partner's energy and well-being. Without boundaries, others unintentionally drain them by overlooking needs or expecting endless flexibility. Boundaries allow them to decide how they want to be treated and how they want to spend their limited energy.

Social Boundaries

Social boundaries are the limits your communication partner establishes around whom they choose to spend time with. These boundaries develop for several reasons. Their hearing loss dictates whose voices are easier to understand. Some family or friends forget to provide natural accommodations (facing them, speaking clearly, avoiding covering their mouth). They naturally gravitate toward certain people at gatherings and avoid others who make communication harder. And spending time with others who also have hearing loss brings comfort and validation through shared experiences.

Experiential Boundaries

Experiential boundaries are the limits your partner sets around how they spend their energy. Each experience demands different levels of:

- Auditory and visual attention

- Cognitive effort to fill in missed information

- Self-disclosure, self-advocacy, and adaptation to communication styles

These boundaries show up in two ways. First, your communication partner declines or leaves experiences that drain more than they give: skipping a concert where noise levels make listening unenjoyable, passing on a large party knowing quiet conversation will be impossible, or declining a dinner invitation because lipreading while people eat is too difficult.

Second, they seek out experiences that feel sustainable: listening to music together at home, inviting a few friends for lunch on the patio, or choosing a quiet coffee shop over a crowded bar. Both are acts of self-protection—one sets limits, the other creates alternatives.

Keep in mind, there's a difference between using boundaries to improve quality of life and using them to avoid meaningful or necessary activities. Help your partner stay intentional, supporting choices that protect energy while still encouraging connection and engagement.

- **Respect choices:** Don't pressure them into draining situations "for fun" if they've set a boundary.

- **Help identify patterns:** Notice which environments leave them energized vs. exhausted.

- **Reinforce value:** Remind them that boundaries aren't selfish; they are healthy.

Ally Insights

- Do I pressure my partner to join events that are hard for them?

- How do I feel when they set a boundary that excludes me too?

- What new traditions or activities could we create that honor their boundaries while keeping us connected?

In *Becoming Hearing Empowered*, your communication partner's journal activity **Boundaries** asks them to:

- Reflect on boundaries they already have.

- Consider boundaries they'd like to establish.

- Think about how boundaries improve their well-being.

Ask:

- "Are there certain people or settings where you'd like me to help protect your boundaries?"

- "How do I tell when you need a break, and what's the best way for me to support that?"

- "Are there any boundaries you'd like us to revisit or strengthen together?"

Section 6 – Other Forms of Self-Care

ALLY PERSPECTIVE: WHY THIS MATTERS

True self-care for your loved one includes more than rest; it's about feeling safe, proud, and connected. By understanding barriers like audism and hearing privilege, supporting hearing protection, celebrating their technology, learning sign language, and encouraging community connections, you help nurture both their confidence and their sense of belonging.

Audism, Ableism, and Hearing Privilege

It's important to understand the social forces that impact your loved one's life. Living with hearing loss is not just about devices or fatigue. It's also about how society views and treats people who can't hear in typical ways.

Audism is discrimination or prejudice against people who are deaf or hard of hearing. It judges, labels, and limits individuals based on whether they hear and speak.

Ableism is discrimination or prejudice against people with disabilities, based on the belief that typical abilities are superior. Both audism and ableism position hearing people as "normal" and those with hearing loss as "less than."

Hearing privilege is the invisible set of advantages that come with having typical hearing. Examples include being able to watch any movie regardless of captioning, attending a doctor's appointment without needing an interpreter, learning spoken language easily as a child, or ordering through a drive-thru without barriers.

For your loved one, encountering audism, ableism, or the effects of hearing privilege feels invalidating, isolating, and exhausting. Recognizing these realities helps you respond with empathy and solidarity rather than unintentionally reinforcing bias.

ALLY IN ACTION

- **Call it out:** If someone dismisses or stereotypes your loved one, speak up respectfully. Don't leave the burden entirely on them.

- **Reflect on privilege:** Notice the things you do easily with hearing that they cannot, and don't take those for granted.

- Do I assume my loved one's barriers are "not a big deal" because they don't affect me?

- How often do I overlook hearing privilege in my daily life?

- Am I willing to speak up when I see audism or ableism in action?

In the *Becoming Hearing Empowered* journal activity **Audism, Ableism, and Hearing Privilege**, your loved one reflects on:

- Times they experienced audism or ableism and how it made them feel.

- People in their life who don't understand hearing privilege, and whether explaining it helps.

- How they counteract these experiences, or whether they feel inspired to become an activist.

Ask:

- "Have you experienced audism or ableism in situations I didn't notice?"

- "How do I support you when you face these kinds of challenges?"

Sign Language as Self-Care

Sign language is a powerful, visual communication system that bypasses hearing altogether. Even if your friend with hearing loss doesn't currently use sign language, learning it is an empowering form of self-care and a meaningful option for communication.

Learning ASL (American Sign Language) with your friend:

- Provides an alternative when spoken communication feels exhausting.

- Creates a deeper connection between you when hearing and speech fall short.

- Opens doors to Deaf culture and community.

Hearing Protection

If your friend with hearing loss has residual hearing, protecting it is critical. Loud noise permanently damages the inner ear. You can help by:

- Encouraging use of hearing protection (earmuffs, custom earplugs, or disposable earplugs).

- Checking potentially harmful sound with decibel level apps.

- Supporting lifestyle changes like lowering TV volume, increasing distance from speakers, or limiting exposure time.

Noise damage occurs much faster than most people realize:

- 85 dB (hair dryer): 8 hours

- 100 dB (subway): 15 minutes

- 130 dB (explosives, aircraft): <1 second

Celebrating Hearing Technology

Beyond acceptance, some people with hearing loss choose to celebrate their devices, using color, skins, stickers, or jewelry to make them an expression of identity. This shifts devices from "medical equipment" to "personal style."

- Support and encourage their self-expression.

- Compliment decorated devices as you would eyewear or clothing.

- Reinforce the message that hearing devices are nothing to hide.

Finding Their People

Connecting with others who also live with hearing loss is one of the most important forms of self-care. You should know that:

- Peer support validates experiences in ways hearing people often cannot.

- Organizations like Hearing Loss Association of America, the National Association of the Deaf, the Association of Late-Deafened Adults, and the Coalition for Global Hearing Health provide community and advocacy.

- Social media and online groups also offer connection and shared resources.

Encouraging your loved one to connect with these communities doesn't replace your support. It adds another layer of understanding and belonging.

Check out **hearingoutloud.net/resources** for links about sign language, creative ways to dress up hearing devices, and for organizations supporting people with hearing loss.

ALLY CONNECTION: BECOMING HEARING EMPOWERED

In *Becoming Hearing Empowered*, your loved one completes the journal activity **Find Your People** and reflects on:

- Whether they already know others with hearing loss.

- How those relationships support them differently than hearing-only ones.

- Whether they'd like to find more connections, and how (organizations, social media, peer groups).

To support them:

- Ask, "Would you like me to help you look for local or online groups?"

- Offer to attend a group or meeting with them.

- Encourage without pressuring. Finding peers should feel like empowerment, not obligation.

Section 7: Your Self-Care

Supporting a loved one with hearing loss is deeply meaningful, but it is also demanding. As you encourage your friend, it's just as important to recognize your own limits and needs. Self-care for you means tending to your identity, protecting your energy, and maintaining a balanced relationship where hearing loss doesn't become the only defining thread. Just as your loved one benefits from setting boundaries, you too need space and balance to stay grounded and connected.

Protecting Your Own Identity

It's easy to let hearing loss become the central focus of your relationship. You may feel as though every outing, conversation, or family event revolves around strategies and accommodations. While hearing loss is significant, it should not eclipse the richness of your shared life. Hold onto your own hobbies, friendships, and pursuits. Continue investing in the parts of your identity that are not tied to being an ally.

Guarding Your Energy

Advocating, educating others, and supporting your loved one takes emotional and mental energy. You don't need to be "on" all the time. Notice when you feel drained or resentful. It may be time to step back, take a quiet break, or engage in activities that refill your own well-being. Protecting your energy is not neglecting your loved one. It is preserving your ability to be present and compassionate over the long term.

Reaching Out for Support

If supporting your friend with hearing loss begins to feel too intense or one-sided, seek out your own support system. This means talking with trusted friends, connecting with other hearing allies, or connecting with professionals like therapists or counselors. Hearing loss affects relationships, and it is normal to need perspective and encouragement from others who understand.

Keeping Balance in the Relationship

Hearing loss will shape your connection, but it should not define it. Create intentional moments where hearing loss is *not* the center of attention. Enjoy a shared hobby, a walk, or time with friends where the focus is on fun and companionship. This balance reminds both of you that your relationship is bigger than the challenges of communication.

Enjoying Events Independently

Some environments, like concerts, sporting events, or noisy social gatherings, may simply be too challenging for your friend. It is okay for you to attend those events without them, if that feels comfortable for your relationship. Giving yourself permission to enjoy these experiences separately prevents resentment and ensures you don't feel you have to sacrifice the things you love.

Expressing Your Own Communication Needs

While much of this book is about supporting your loved one's communication, you also have needs of your own. Perhaps you need time to decompress after work before diving into conversation, want to enjoy background music while cooking, or crave an evening with friends where you're not the communication bridge. Maybe you need space to feel frustrated without guilt, or permission to not have all the answers. These needs are valid. Communicating them openly creates a healthier, more reciprocal relationship.

- **Protect your identity:** Identify one hobby or activity that helps you feel like yourself, apart from being an ally, and commit to practicing it regularly.

- **Honor the signals:** Notice moments of resentment or fatigue and treat them as signals to rest and replenish, not as failures.

- **Connect beyond hearing loss:** Create intentional times with your loved one where hearing loss is not the focus.

ALLY INSIGHTS

- Do I feel like hearing loss dominates our relationship?

- How do I recharge my own energy when supporting my loved one feels heavy?

- Who do I reach out to for my own support and perspective?

Closing

You have completed the final chapter of *Becoming an Empowered Hearing Ally: A Guide for Family, Friends, and Allies of People with Hearing Loss.* By walking through these pages, you've not only gained knowledge; you've become a more supportive ally. You have learned that hearing loss is not just about missing sounds, but about navigating a world where communication requires effort, understanding, and advocacy. And you've discovered that you have a powerful role to play in making that journey easier, more dignified, and more empowering for your loved one.

ALLY INSIGHTS – FINAL REFLECTION

Reflect on your thoughts and feelings now that you've completed this book.

- What have you learned about hearing loss that surprised you?

- How do you hope this book will change the way you support your loved one?

- Are there sections you'd like to revisit or practice again together?

- How do you see yourself continuing to grow as an empowered hearing ally?

ACKNOWLEDGEMENTS

This book has landed in your hands with the help and support of people who shared their time, talent, and encouragement along the way.

To **Kaitlin Walsh**, my cover artist—thank you for beautifully translating the heart of this book into watercolor with such depth and sensitivity.

To the **Early Ally Readers**—thank you for the time you spent providing thoughtful feedback and honest reflections during the early stages of this project. Your insights helped refine the message behind these pages.

And to **you**, the reader—thank you for taking the time to step into the role of an ally.

ABOUT THE AUTHOR

Katherine S. Rybak, M.Ed., NBCT, was born Hard of Hearing and is the founder of Hearing Out Loud®, an organization dedicated to empowering people with hearing loss and their allies. Through her work, Katherine helps others embrace identity, maximize technology, and confidently advocate for communication access in every part of life.

A retired Teacher of the Deaf and Hard of Hearing, Katherine holds a master's degree in education and is a National Board Certified Teacher. She brings together lived experience, professional expertise, and creative vision to support people with hearing loss—and to guide friends, family, and professionals to become better hearing allies.

Katherine and her wife Carol live in Madison, Wisconsin, where they enjoy time with their three grown children. She finds joy in traveling with family, creative projects in her studio, and playful moments with her grandchildren.

Also by Katherine S. Rybak

For teens and adults:

- *Becoming Hearing Empowered: A Guided Journal for the Deaf and Hard of Hearing*

Chapter books for kids (ages 8–12)

- *A Little Mic, A Big Change*

- *Signs on the Court* (coming May 2026)

- More stories coming soon!

Resources

For free resources, including book study guides, a professional guide, a hearing ally cheat sheet, videos, and links to organizations and technology, visit **hearingoutloud.net/hearing-ally**